ManagementOne

Pieter H Henning

A practical guide to managing people

Forward

Middle management and Supervisors spend most of the money in the organisation, even if they do not write or sign the cheques. They apply the raw materials, use the spare parts, manage the resources and the staff. This group of managers is responsible for making the products and therefore actually manufactures the income. They are normally the least equipped and most overseen group in management. They need all the help they can get.

This book will deal with the basic skills that you need to be a manager. There are many tips and discussions on what is required and how to deal with the demands you may face. This is a practical guide of what to do to affect tomorrow by doing something today. If management is a vehicle, this would be a driving course with some advanced driving lessons rather than technical training on the workings of the engine and electrical systems of the car. You can be an excellent driver without knowing how the engine actually works. The same applies to management.

The style in which this book has been written is that of telling and sharing - much in the form of a lecture - to make it more interesting. This is a practical guide; apply it and experiment with the ideas and concepts until they work for you and for the environment you're in.

You will venture into areas that some scholars and professional scientists have reserved for themselves. Do not fear going there. You will find it far more familiar than you thought possible. Any person can study nature and has been doing so since the first person that walked the earth. This is what science is. You may call yourself a scientist if you formulate and describe a natural phenomenon or behaviour. If you really think about it, we are all scientists. Babies observe gravity, for example, when they drop something. Their theories are repeated with great success as parents repeatedly pick up the things that they throw down to make sure gravity is still working as they have formulated it. We do not know what they call it, but they certainly know what gravity is, even if they do not know that the object that falls from their hands accelerates at 9.81 metres per second squared. Babies also know that if they do certain things it brings great joy to their parents. This is an observation of behavioural patterns. Is a baby a scientist? Are you a scientist because you observe nature and think about it and act accordingly? Sure you are.

Once you have studied and applied the teachings of this book, you will observe your surroundings from a new angle and make some useful observations of your own that are not covered in this book. Do not stop here. Once you have read this book I recommend that you read and study many other books. Observe more, read more and learn more to understand and apply the subjects on Management and people.

Gender references in the book:
In the chapters of this book, I will refer to "he" or "him" or "his" when I refer to a person. This reference is applicable to both male and female and I have used the masculine pronouns for practical reasons only.

ManagementOne
~ Contents ~

Most of a manager's day can consist of solving some kind of problem. Most problems are easy to solve, but every so often there is a "show stopper" that needs to be solved properly and quickly. You can solve problems effectively if you apply a strategy.

The organisation that you work for and the country that you work in have rules and regulations that need to be honoured and respected. Your staff may disregard these rules, resulting in your department performing poorly. How do you deal with those who refuse to honour the rules?

I thank all the wonderful people who invested their time and efforts into my life and this book. This includes YOU!

A final word regarding Management and Engineering. Enjoy it!

Getting started as a Manager

I can clearly remember my first formal job as a Supervisor. I had recently qualified as an Engineer and was completely out of my depth managing other people to achieve the results expected of the team. I had been managing processes and people before, but I had never been appointed in this role. Needless to say, it was not a time in my life that I would like to repeat and I regret the errors I made during this time. After this ordeal, I changed careers for a short while and sold insurance, where I effectively worked for myself for commission only. I actually had to manage myself. This was a fantastic learning curve in management since I was on both ends of every experiment, argument and technique as I tried to get myself to perform at my best and bring home some money. In the end I got it to work, but hankered back to the job-satisfaction of engineering, so I resigned on a high note and returned to engineering, where my passion was and still is.

I hope your experience as a manager or supervisor will be much better than mine, and that you will be a more effective manager as a result of the information and skills that you will find in the chapters of this book. If you are already in a management position and find it difficult to cope, you can take a quick look through the index and determine which chapters you need to read first in order to make immediate improvements. Eventually you will have to study each chapter to be able to deal with most of the aspects of your job as a manager. You will acquire the basic skills and knowledge from this book if you study and practice each chapter. Please make sure that you apply the knowledge carefully, with the emphasis on apply. Knowledge in the wrong hands can be like a child with a gun. Some of you may have had such a manager and all of us know how bad that was.

Managers versus Leaders:
Before you read the rest of the book I would like to clarify the difference between leadership and management. This is important since you will most likely read and study other books to get more information and skills to improve yourself beyond the basics of this book. You will come across books on both subjects. I recommend you read and study both subjects for neither one can be studied or applied in isolation.

By my definition, a leader has followers. It is as simple as that. Think about it for a while: if he has a vision and a goal and if they want to follow him there, the leader walks in front and the people behind him will follow, through free will, to where he leads them. They will only willingly follow him if they trust him. A leader influences people to follow him.

A manager manages people and resources to achieve a specific goal. Nobody follows a manager, they are in front of him and he pushes them and steers them to where he wants them to be, not where they necessarily want to be.

Think of the difference in a simple parable. Think of a flock of sheep. A leader is the shepherd who walks in front, calling the sheep to follow, which they will do if they know and trust him. A manager is like a sheep dog, running behind and driving the sheep forward using fear, barking and biting to keep them moving in the direction he wants them to go.

It is, of course, not as simple as this since you need to do a bit of leading and managing almost all the time. Sometimes your staff will follow your lead and other times you will have to force them to do something. This book will deal with both subjects from the manager's point of view, without necessarily defining which is which every time it deals with the issue. Here is a statement to think about and debate amongst your peers: "A good leader is a servant to those he leads, otherwise he is just a manager".

Your actual task as a manager:
The one difference between a worker and a manager is that the worker does the work and the manager makes sure the worker does the work. Your job as a manager is not to do the work of the workers. This concept will surface everywhere in this book. Do not misunderstand this concept. A manager is certainly working, but he does not do the work of the people he manages. If he does, he will be in trouble. In the example above, where there are sheep being managed, neither the shepherd, nor the dog, are sheep. You too must be different from the workers you manage. There must be a clear distinction between you and the workers.

Your journey of knowledge, starting now:
There are a few things you need to realise at this point:

a. You need to gain knowledge on the subject of management.

b. You need to implement and practice the knowledge.

c. You also need skills and experience, together with knowledge, to perform better in your job as supervisor or manager.

Many senior managers have told me that the number one reason that they have problems with the performance of their staff is incompetence. I want to agree with this statement simply because of my own experience. In order to get to a position where you have competence and confidence you have to ask others for help. Read books on the subject and train yourself and your workers almost all the time. (I'm sure you agree, since you are reading this book).

The process of learning a new skill is summed up in four steps:

1. You do not know that you do not know.
2. You realise that there is a lot to learn and this is when you know that you do not know.
3. You know that you know.
4. You do not know that you know. This is where you want to be, when you can perform your work without constantly thinking about the technicalities of your work.

The Social Sciences refer to these stages as:

1. Unconsciously incompetent
2. Consciously incompetent
3. Consciously competent
4. Unconsciously competent

You need to get to the forth stage where you will be doing the right thing without thinking about it. To understand this better, think of a driver of a car. In the beginning the driver experiences a lot of stress when negotiating traffic. After a few years he will negotiate busy streets and shift gears, use the indicator, consider other traffic and so on without constantly concentrating on each action. You can test this by asking the driver what he just did after changing gears and I assure you the answer will not be what you expect.

There will always be new ideas and new things to learn. You will have to read articles in magazines, read books, take part in discussions and much more if you want to equip yourself and invest in your career to excel as a manager. Every time you find out about a new skill you will go through the other three stages before you can claim that you have mastered the new skill.

Your first tasks as a manager in a new position:
In the early 80s my girlfriend's father attended a management course at his place of work. (Yes, I married her!) He sat with the books and files on the dining room table trying to study by teaching me, his future son-in-law. I remember two things from that Sunday afternoon: "Piet, what are the most important tasks on your list when you walk into a new job as a manager?" And the answer followed when I failed to answer it correctly: "Listen carefully as this is important: 1) you must establish good communication channels both up and down and 2) you must take stock and record the present condition and situation". Good advice indeed!

Task 1: Communication:
Your position is in relationship to the senior person that you report to, to the other managers on your level who also report to that person and to the staff reporting to you. You must therefore have an open communication channel up, down and sideways with other departments related to the section of the organisation that you manage. Do not assume anything. Ask the relevant superiors and peers how they want you to communicate with them. They will tell you. If they throw the question back, tell them how you would like to communicate with them, for example:

☞ To a service department, like maintenance, you will want to communicate with formal written documents like job cards and you want formal reports every day or week on the status of each job and maintenance plans.

☞ With the finance department you want a report on the expenditure under your "cost centres" or budgets every month with a flag system to notify you of spending without your signature or if the amount is more than what was agreed on.

☞ With your superior or manager you will report on the targets and how you achieved them, plans to improve and actions taken during the month to stop problems caused by unforeseen issues. Do not make excuses or do blame-fixing, but focus on solutions.

☞ Find out what reporting systems are presently used and determine if they are sufficient or not. Evaluate this in terms of what the end user needs and if the end user actually uses the information. Try not to get busier with reporting the work than actually doing the work on which you report.

☞ Think carefully about each department before you discuss the matter with them.

☞ Apart from the above, there will be formal or standard reports that are part of the process and production.

> You can ponder over yesterday, you can plan something for tomorrow, but you can only do something today.

Task 2: Taking stock of the present situation:
Taking stock of the present situation before you start managing is important because you need to know what exactly it is that you face. Every task that involves people will be different because of the nature of each person.

You need to:

1. Understand where the problems are, and where things work well.

2. Test the level of knowledge of the people in terms of the product, process, plant and machines. Hopefully there will be tests available for this. If not, ask a senior person to help you draw up some tests from the manuals.

3. Evaluate the condition of the equipment. If you cannot do this, ask someone to help. Your superior should be able to do a walk-about and discuss each machine, plant or section.

4. Record and evaluate statistics related to turnover, production, waste, failure rates, scrap rates, breakdowns, staff turnover and other important numbers.

5. Take photos of the plant, if it is practical, to get a proper record of housekeeping, plant condition and so forth.

Make sure you talk to all parties involved when you do this. It will be expected of you to improve the section under your control. To measure the improvement you need to know from where you started. Make sure what improvement is expected of you and quantify it. Set the target or benchmark and communicate it to both your superior and your staff so that everybody has the same expectations. If you do not quantify the goal in relation to the present condition, the goal posts will move all the time and the formal reward will dangle like a big carrot in front of you forever. If you do quantify it, you will get to eat the carrot every now and then, before getting a bigger one to keep the challenge alive.

The daily test:
A while ago my eldest son Hendrik, then sixteen years old, came to me with a test paper in his hand. He told me that it was the Mathematics test he had written earlier that day and that he had done well. He showed me the problems he could solve and those he had got wrong. I asked him why he was sure how he had done if the test was not yet marked, His answer got me thinking long after our conversation ended. He told me that he was prepared for the test and that he went over the test after school and checked every answer he gave earlier, spotting his errors. He used the test as an opportunity to learn.

So why did it get me thinking? Simple: I asked myself how I had done that day in my test called WORK.

☞ Was I prepared?

☞ Did I look back over every problem to make sure the answer was right?

☞ Did I learn from the events of that day?

Of course I had not done all of that on that particular day!

This does not mean that I had failed as a manager, just that I had missed out on the opportunity to learn from that day and plan for the next. Most successful people have the good habit of taking stock at the end of every day, learning from it and planning the next day.

> TODAY is the first day of the rest of your life or the first day of the rest of the project, the problem, the task or whatever it is you are doing.

Disappointment:

Disappointment, as I define it, is the difference between what you expect and the reality. Make sure you know and understand what is expected of you because you cannot always control it. You will have to ask if you are not 100% sure of what is expected of you and the work your team must do. The part of the definition you must make happen is the reality. The expectation can be re-negotiated if you know the reality will not reach it. This way your superior will not be as disappointed, but will be in a position to help you or provide assistance in some form so that you can achieve the original goal. In the same way, your staff needs to know what is expected of them so that they can realise their part in order to avoid disappointment from you. You must communicate the goals and results all the time and influence them to deliver what you expect.

Later in the book we will look at the subject of disappointment again with more emphasis on managing the disappointment from your staff.

Blame-fixing:
In my career as a senior manager I was the victim of a blame-fixing culture almost all the time and can truly say I have worked for very few Managers or Directors who did not allow it. It is very easy to let a blame-fixing or "kindergarten" culture develop. Yes, it is exactly a "kindergarten" culture that does not belong in an adult world.

You must guard against it with all your strength so that it does not develop in the area under your supervision. Here are some rules you need to keep in order to be a good manager with regards to a blaming culture:

☞ Never listen and agree when one person blames the other for his non-performance.

☞ If you find the root cause for a person's non-performance, focus on the problem and not on the person.

☞ If you find out a person could have prevented a non-performance you must offer help and assistance. Follow up and ensure that the person has gained the necessary knowledge and experience to prevent a re-occurrence of the non-performance.

☞ If one of your staff members has the habit of fixing blame you must interrupt the person as soon as you realise that blame is being fixed and ask him a direct question: "Did you help that person with the possible problem when you saw it and so prevent it?" In this way the culture will change.

☞ If somebody carries stories and blame-fixing to you, stop the conversation and call the person being discussed or blamed to join the conversation so that the rest of the story can be told in the other person's presence. This will catch the blamer unaware and he will have to be very careful as to what he says. The habit will soon stop.

For the record, my wife studied and became a kindergarten teacher after our children were teenagers and had good experience with the tricks and minds of a child. It took only a few weeks in the beginning of each year to stop the blaming culture that the young boys and girls had when they reported to school. To stop it she followed the rules above. Teachers who fail to do this spend hours every day sorting out who did what to whom. Because the teacher listened and paid the blamers undeserved attention, those hours are wasted forever and the children will come with more and more blaming every day.

Honesty:

If a manager has measles, his staff will not have chickenpox. This was the advice from a friend of mine in my early 30s. If you are dishonest, your staff will be dishonest. You expect honesty from your staff. You expect them to respect others and do their work with integrity. They are not allowed to steal from you, and this includes time, spares, stock, cash from the till, etc. This means you must not steal from them, must respect them, be honest and be a model worker.

You are the one who sets the example.

If you are dishonest and think you can outsmart your staff, your suppliers or your customers so that they will not know it, you are an idiot. (I say this with respect).

My late father used to tell me that he would never sell his name for all the money in the world. As a young person it made no sense when he told me that. I grew up in a fairly protected environment and corruption, bribes and shady deals were not something I was exposed to, yet my father, in his wisdom, prepared me for my adult life. Since I have been working I have seen people selling their names and, by default, the company name, for a contract, or a commission or something trivial, like being noticed, without blinking. You will have to stand firm. Being honest is no easy job if others in the company are not, especially if they are your seniors and you must uphold or manage the lie.

Staff turnover:

The best feedback you can get about your ability to manage people is your staff turnover. I'm not talking about the few that resign when you establish your section because you may shuffle things a bit when you start. Once you are settled you do not want a big staff turnover. The best way to explain this is to extract from a blog:

Why People Quit People, Not Companies:

According to Chapter 16 of the book Leadership Gold by John Maxwell, "People Quit People, Not Companies". The author mentioned a few general reasons for this, and some of the contents of the chapter are captured in the page "Find Out the Reason of High Manpower Turnover" [*1]. As I reflected and did further research on this subject, I stumbled upon a quote here [*2] saying "Power Plus Incompetence Equals a Mean Boss". True enough, but this is just the beginning. I realised there are many dangerous combinations that may equate to a really bad boss.

* Power plus Incompetence
* Competence plus Insecurity
* Communication plus Distrustfulness
* Vision plus Inconsistency
* Generosity plus Favouritism
* Optimism plus Close-Mindedness
* Courage plus Arrogance
* Passion without Values
* Knowledge without Focus
* Position without Accountability
* Goals without Plans
* Instructions without Reasons
* Speed without Adaptability
* Experiences without Growth

Responsible employees who notice these signs within their organisation, try to help out or do something to improve things. But, at the end of the day, if they've done what they can but don't see actual improvements or even just the desire to improve on the part of their boss or manager, they tend to leave the organisation. Since their boss or manager is obviously naturally self-destructing, they just wish them luck and leave him alone.

Addresses of blog and links:
*body: http://epc-thethirdview.blogspot.com/2010/05/why-people-quit-people-not-companies.html
*1:   http://leaderboss.com/leaders-mindset/find-out-the-reason-of-high-manpower-turnover/
*2:   http://www.newsweek.com/id/218460
Note: The picture was changed to gray scale because there is only one colour used for printing this book.

Whenever a worker resigns, make sure you have an exit interview with that person. It may be better if a colleague conducts the interview so that the worker can speak more freely and you will get honest reasons. Use the information you get from the exit interview and learn from it so that you can improve yourself as a manager. If accusations were made against you, you must look into it carefully and learn from it. Staff turnover is a big problem. Each good or valued worker that leaves creates a problem that the rest of team must absorb until that worker is replaced and trained. This is also costly. Prevent it "at all cost".

What do you do with a worker who seems to have more management ability than yourself? Firstly, do not be intimidated or threatened by it. Secondly, give him more responsibility and, thirdly, make sure your superior knows this and will be on the lookout for a higher position in the company for this worker. If you do not do this, the worker will be frustrated and leave.

Reading a book is easy. Learning from it is also easy. Implementing what you learn needs motivation and effort. The questions at the end of the chapters are there to help you.

Ask yourself the following and check the correct box:

	Yes	No
Do I lie to my staff about their performance?	☐	☐
Do I lie to my staff about their value to the company?	☐	☐
Do I underpay any of my staff?	☐	☐
Do I give honest reviews?	☐	☐

	Yes	No
Do I abuse my staff in terms of their time?	☐	☐
Do I offer bribes to ensure deals?	☐	☐
Do I take bribes from suppliers to ensure they get orders?	☐	☐
Do I lie about the performance of our products to get sales?	☐	☐
Do I steal time from the company?	☐	☐

If you answered yes to any of these questions you can fix it by doing the following: STOP IT !!

Make a list of all you have done wrong and undo them one by one.

Bring it to light and ask forgiveness. If you can, repay them or fix the damage.

If your company expects you to be dishonest, tell them you are not willing to do it. Depending on their reaction you may want to seek other employment.

2

Manage the inputs

So many managers do not realise this concept that it can almost be considered a secret. I found out about it the hard way when I worked for commission without a basic pay: I was working hard and did not earn any money for it. I had to look into the way I managed the business. Later I found that non-salaried and business owners (working for yourself or commission only) know much more about the concept than those who gets a regular paycheque, regardless of the results of their work.

> "Manage the inputs and demand results."

Simple, is it not? So why do so few managers practise it? I have no idea why Business Schools and mentors teach the most sophisticated theories, some of which are "patented", while they fail to teach this simple concept.

Advantages and disadvantages:

Some people demand results without helping the person who must deliver these results. Study the lists below to see the advantages of the one and disadvantages of the other.

Advantages of "Managing the inputs":

☞ You can get the worker to do whatever it is that will deliver the desired result.

☞ You can assist in achieving the above and therefore be in control of the process.

☞ You can monitor the execution of the inputs as they happen.

☞ You can get a report of what inputs were made before the output is achieved and make changes or add something in order to get the desired result and affect the input effort, quality, quantity and timing at an early stage.

☞ You can forecast the results if you keep statistics over a long period. You can also use this the other way round and determine exactly what input is needed for a specific result.

☞ You can request reports daily or at very short intervals and make immediate adjustments to the type or frequency of the inputs.

☞ You can help or get more workers or other help when you see some help is needed with inputs.

☞ Experts can list the inputs to achieve results for complex work that you do not understand and you can make sure the inputs are done at pre-agreed intervals, even if you cannot do the work yourself.

Disadvantages of "Managing the results":

☞ By the time the result are out, there is absolutely nothing you can do to change it. It is history.

☞ Most people start looking for excuses and others to blame to explain the result if it is not the desired one. Very few will examine the inputs to make an effort to change it. I once had a manager who, for more than three years, allowed blaming on a daily basis in the production meetings without addressing the inputs, even after I suggested it to him.

☞ Your superiors will demand a repeat of good results and you will not know how to achieve it.

☞ If you do not know the specific process or task, you can be fooled as to why the results were not achieved and may not be able to prevent a repeat of the poor results.

☞ You will end up threatening your staff to produce better results without any guarantees that they will or can do it the next time they try.

Case study: Engineering breakdown and downtime:

One of my jobs as Engineering Manager was to manage the unplanned breakdowns to below 5% for the entire factory. I achieved this by applying the "Manage the inputs and demand results" method. We had a new computerised maintenance system. Maintenance was scheduled per machine section and much more. All work done by artisans was recorded. I made sure they did the scheduled maintenance or, if the machines were not available, they had to do inspections and raise job cards against all faults or potential problems. There were several other inputs that resulted in machines being repaired before they broke down. The resulting downtime figures were issued by the secretary who summarised the production reports, not by the staff reporting to me. In ten months the downtime was reduced from almost 8% to 1.8% of available production time. My role in that achievement was to monitor and manage the inputs while my competent staff did the actual work that resulted in such a low unplanned downtime.

What do we learn from this story?

- Inputs do not necessary produce immediate results.

- The inputs will definitely give results if the inputs are done by the people who are responsible for it.

- Your inputs may be another person's job. Manage it well and results will follow.

- Never let the same person monitor the inputs and the results. It may be adjusted to look good.

Case study: The wire fence:

As a small boy I used to throw stones through a meshed wire fence. The mesh was about 5cm or 2 inches. I threw stones the size of a marble. No matter how carefully I threw, the stone would touch or strike the fence at least six out of ten times, even though there was a lot more hole than fence. I concluded it was a law of nature. Until this day I periodically throw a few stones at a fence when I get the chance, to see if the theory holds up. It does, without fail.

So what did I do to eventually get ten out of ten stones through the fence? I managed to get ten out of ten stones through the wire without touching it by standing against the fence and pushing the stones through.

So why do I share this experience?:

- In your work there will be a few obvious things to do, yet you will find the result is not what you expected.

- You can try until you die of old age to get it right or you can determine the natural tendency and manage a counter approach to break the rhythm, apply a process to create new starts and so forth.

- You can control what goes in so that the desired outcome is achieved.

Practical exercise:

Make a list of the outputs you must achieve, or that the people working for you must achieve. Next to each output, write what inputs you must ensure to achieve the output. See sample below:

Output or Result	Inputs TODAY	Comments
500 sets of three types of shoes per day	Prepare mould changes. Prepare machine setting changes. Check availability of different raw materials.	One mould in workshop. We will have it by 18h00. Other inputs =Done

Scrap less than 0.2%	Assist operator with new glue gun. Ask Supervisor to assist with raw material checks. Ask maintenance to re-tune the stitching machine.	Operator scheduled for extra training during mould changes. Maintenance is on standby with relevant tools.

Never give up:

Sometimes doing the right thing all the time without getting the right results taps your energy. Do not let this get you down, because you will start managing the results, watching the outcome and, if it is not the desired one, you will discipline the workers. I have seen this happen many times. Never give up managing the inputs. Never give up hope. If what you do does not work, change the angle, break the objective down into smaller pieces and manage those smaller inputs. Ask for help. The end result is your objective, not the process.

In the previous chapter I made the statement: "TODAY is the TOMORROW of YESTERDAY", this means today you are seeing and experiencing the results of the inputs you made yesterday. Not doing this is a little bit like the lumberjack who does not have time to sharpen his axe and gets more and more behind every day.

> You can affect tomorrow today. The moment you realise that you cannot, you must stop everything and start over, rethink, break down the process in small steps that you understand and can manage.

Checks to make sure you have the benefit of this chapter:

Put dates after each statement. Come back and tick them
off when you have done what you have committed to do.

I will find out what the results or targets are and note
the inputs I must make that will affect the results directly
and indirectly by: __ /__ /__ ☐

I will test the staff to see if they understand what inputs
gives the result for which they are responsible by: __ /__ /__ ☐

I will demand the desired results; make sure that the staff
plans the inputs and assist them so that they can achieve
the results by: __ /__ /__ ☐

Although helping a person does not mean that I will do
the actual work, I will put in place systems to measure
the inputs and help the staff as soon as they slip by: __ /__ /__ ☐

3

Your responsibilities

You are at your desk on the first day of your new management job. What exactly must you do? If you are a manager, who must you manage, what are their names? What processes are you responsible for and what work do the workers do? You must know all this in great detail. The company or person who hired you must tell you. You must know what the people you manage must do and then you must manage them.

The way to define your responsibilities is by means of KPA's (Key Performance Areas) or Key performance Indicators (KPI) or Key Result Areas (KRA). I prefer to use Key Performance Area because it is easier to explain. The result is the same, no matter what method you use. The method I use here to explain responsibilities is KPA because an "AREA on a map" is something a person can see. It is a tool to explain what the department or individual must do and what outcome is desired by the organisation he works for.

KPAs tell you what goals to achieve, not how to achieve the goals. It is your job description and the reason why you are hired. It is a management tool to guide you, help you and assess your work rationally. This book will deal with that as much as possible. You must have KPAs for yourself as well as each one of your staff. It may be possible for your staff who work in groups to have the same KPAs. What you learn must be applied to all situations. KPAs are also the tool that will be used to assess your performance.

Exercise: Take a sheet of clean paper and write down what you know as your key tasks, then put them on a "map" in relation to others from whom you get work and to whom you pass on work.

In the many years I have worked for others, I had one or two managers who used KPAs more or less correctly.

> Warning:
>
> Please use this KPA tool correctly or you may have unmotivated staff.

Case Study: KPAs

Before we get into too much detail about this subject, let me share an experience that convinced me to investigate my KPAs.

In 1987 I was an insurance salesman. The work was interesting and took a lot of my time. When I was recruited the average salary of the more or less 3210 Salesmen in the company was ZAR2800 per month. This was a good salary for a young man at that time. What they did not tell us was that the top ten salesmen earned about 50% of all the commissions and if you removed those ten from the statistics the average for the other nearly 3200 representatives with half the total income dropped dramatically to around ZAR1404 per month. I soon found that I was working extremely hard to get almost no money and sometimes I had to pay in or go on credit to pay for the use of the phone, the diaries we handed out, the stationary and so on. It was a real bum deal we had, that was for sure, paying for our office, phone, stationary etc. I had to make a special effort to see why I had such a small paycheque and why I often had to thank my wife for supporting us. I started recording everything I did for a week. I soon saw that I was very busy with a lot of work not directly related to receiving a paycheque. I noted down my core tasks, those directly related to a paycheque and started doing those first and for a while I actually did only the core tasks during working hours. The other tasks were done on weekends and after hours. My income soon picked up and reached an average far above the average of the company. I understood what my money-generating tasks were and performed those tasks first. In this process some colleagues helped me with the actual skills and schemes to find prospects and close more deals. I managed the inputs and the results followed like "magic".

Many other colleagues struggled with the same problem and left the company, sad and broke, to find other employment. Our manager used to send some of the others to me with the instruction to go and see how I applied the "basics" in order to get and close sales. My advice was sometimes too simple for some of them. They would probably have preferred some "intelligent" answer with many fancy words and theories.

I no longer sell insurance, but since that time I have always asked what I should do first, today or right now, that will bring profit to the owners of the company I work for. Note, I say "profit" and not "money": there is a big difference between money and profit. Your job is also to prevent money being wasted or misused. This is why you are employed, to generate profits for the owners. Always imagine that the company is yours to help you grasp this concept better. Maybe it is yours, anyway.

Key Performance Areas (KPAs):

As I explained in the introduction of this chapter, there are several versions of the way to describe what a person or department must do. I prefer to use KPA to explain it because I find it effective.

A key area is an area on a business map or, expressed another way, a portion of your duties that are listed together on the document that describes what the company is doing. The word "KEY" refers to "Principal" or "main" and means that the "AREA" is a part of the business that cannot be left out, in the same way that you cannot drive around in your car without its key. These key areas are directly related to activities to achieve the core goal of the organisation you work for, which is most likely to deliver a product or service in exchange for money. These duties are called areas because the business of the organisation is normally mapped out in the form of a flow diagram, an organogram or some document to show the responsibilities of each department in the organisation. This means there must be a business map or other descriptive document for your KPAs to make sense. If there is no map, make sure you understand the business enough to see where you fit in and what it is you must do by asking your seniors.

"PERFORMANCE" determines how you are doing and there will be a measurement to assess you against goals set for you by your manager. In most big businesses KPAs are a formal process. In smaller businesses KPAs may be informal and are sometimes not done at all. If not formally in existence, this does not mean you can ignore them. Make your KPA list and measure yourself against it so that you can improve all the time.

Case study: The disciplinary hearing of a supervisor:

This story is about a supervisor who got promoted from within the company; let's call him "John".

John was a reliable and very good machine operator - always on time, always present, even in times of urgent jobs during weekends and public holidays. He had many years of experience in the processes and understood them well. He had worked on other sections in the department and had been exposed to the entire process as well as all the machines. When the opportunity came for a promotion, he applied and was appointed Supervisor. This meant more responsibility and more money. Everybody was happy… for a while.

About six months into his new job, I was called as an observing manager to a hearing where John was accused of not performing his duties. In the hearing it became known that he had indeed not done what was expected of him, but he was under the impression that he was doing well, apart from this one mistake. He told the meeting how hard he worked, so much so that most days he never took his lunch hour and only had the occasional cup of tea on the run. On that particular day he had neglected an important duty because he was assisting an operator with his work by driving the crane and simply did not have time for anything else.

He was the typical person I described in the introduction. In that meeting I volunteered to teach him and give him guidance into the knowledge and skills of management.

My guidance to him was some of what is covered in this book. He became a star performer over the next three months after a few hours of instruction.

What do we learn from this story?

- You are not hired to be busy, but to produce results.

- Avoid the activity trap. John did it and was very surprised at the summary of his activity recordings and made some adjustments to his daily routine.

- Your subordinates will take advantage of you as soon as they see you are willing to do some of their work.

- You must not take over a task if someone struggles with it, you should use the opportunity to teach and give experience. Remember: experience is caught, not taught.

- If you juggle many balls, get some tools to assist you. (See the chapter on Management Tools for this)

- You get what you measure. Measure the output. Do it so that all can see.

- Make sure you also measure skills and performance and retrain those who struggle to perform their duties.

Here's an example to illustrate a KPA:

A warehouse supervisor receives and despatches goods. Is this right? >>>>> No, it is wrong!!!

He does receive goods and he does despatch them, but he probably does the following:

☞ He gets a copy of an order from the buying department to match with a delivery that will come.

☞ If a delivery come he compares the delivery note with the order to see if it was ordered.

☞ He counts the goods to verify that everything on the delivery note is actually delivered.

☞ He notifies the Quality Control department of the arrival of the goods if they need to approve it.

☞ When he gets the approval from QC, he stores the goods in the correct place.

☞ He completes the documentation and sends it to the Finance department to be paid.

☞ He informs the originator of the purchase request that the goods are available.

☞ If he gets a "stores requisition" for the goods, he checks if the approval on the form is in order and issues the goods.

☞ He enters the issued goods into the system (either a note to finance or a management software).

If he has a map of what happens to the materials and information, and he knows the area he is responsible for, then he will understand all the aspects of his work and how it interacts with and affects other areas. He can now explode the map of his area into a lot of detail to show the area of each of his workers. On the next page is a basic map for this manager.

Note:

If you are new to this topic, read through the following pages to get an overview and come back to this point.

The rules for effective personal KPA descriptions are:

1. Draw the business's core function from start to finish. For example, if you manufacture products, draw the raw materials from delivery, past the warehouse, into production. Then draw the produced goods into the stock and from there onto a delivery vehicle.

2. All the activities of the company must be indicated on the map. For example, somewhere on the map will be "order raw material" and from there a line to "store raw material" and from there a hold area where the goods will wait for Quality Control department to approve it for example: "QC check - raw material". From there "issue raw material to production" and so on. If you are working in QC, you will clearly know what to do if you are told to QC the raw material and you will understand how you can affect the total plan if you are in sync with all the work to be done.

3. The area should be relevant to the purpose of the company and must have a DIRECT influence on the core goal of the company.

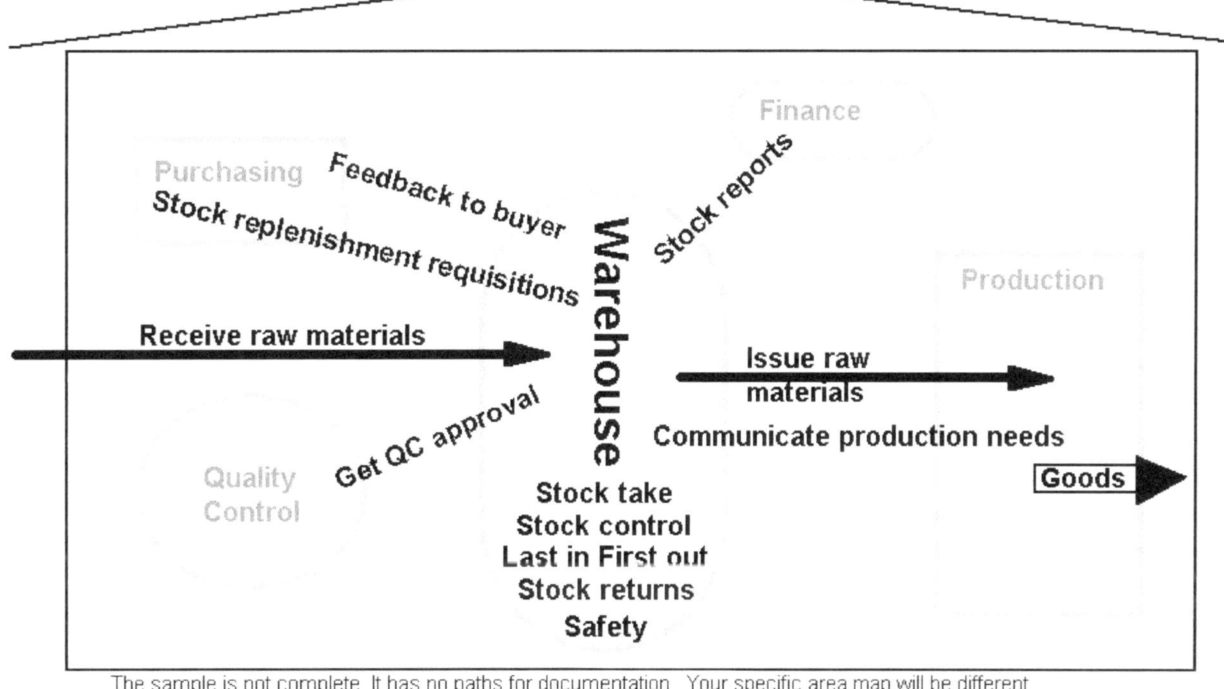

The sample is not complete. It has no paths for documentation. Your specific area map will be different.

4. Every area that you are responsible for must be indicated on the business map.

5. Every area needs a goal or target outcome. These are normally the inputs to the next area and can be actual material or goods. Note we refer here to the outcome for your KPA, not the method for getting there.

6. Every target or goal must be measurable in terms of quantity, percentage, rate, ratio, time or dates. There must be no estimates or perception of the outcome. All measurements must be factual and measurable.

7. The area is in relationship to other areas with inputs and deliverables.

8. Every area needs your agreement on the goal and the outcome to be measured. Do not agree on something that you know cannot be achieved by yourself. In this case you have to agree on the area and its goals, but not that you will achieve it on your own if you cannot. Negotiate a level of assistance and training, plus who must assist you, in order to achieve the goal. Remember that the area's work and its goals needs to be achieved whether you can do it or not. So get help, but get it done.

9. There must be a set date to review your performance against each area. This date must be related to prior dates where the results of each measured task is available. Do not walk into a review meeting without the results of every measured area or task. If you do not have it you'll be at a disadvantage and will soon have to agree that you did not perform to expected standards based on perceptions and hearsay. The same goes for your workers. Measure them against set parameters and report the results to them before the meeting.

10. There must be a set interval period for each review. The longest period between reviews must not exceed six months. This way you can correct actions before the goals are missed completely.

  ManagementOne

It can be informal, as long as you can flag a problem and make a correction in reaching the goal of each area if you struggle. Keep a record of this review, even if it is informal.

11. The purpose of KPAs is to make sure that the areas are managed properly. The review is to determine if an individual reached the set goals and must have the objective of assisting that person if he is not achieving any one of the goals to the expected level.

12. The KPAs must have weights. This means that some KPAs are more important than others and you must direct more energy towards them. I say this because there will most likely be KPAs not linked to the core business of the company and you must be clear about its weight. I prefer to call these "Personal goals" rather than KPAs. This can be for things like conduct, managing absenteeism, reduction in staff turn-over, etc.

> Do not be dishonest with your staff when you review their KPAs. The long term effect outlives the short term triumph by a lifetime.

To Do:

☞ Draw a map of the complete business as best you can. Follow the guidelines from the above points.

☞ Now look again at your 'Area' on the map and add as much detail as you can, almost like putting a magnifying glass on it.

☞ Be very specific and write the flow of information on a line that shows the direction and flow of the information, like I did in the example above for "Communicate production needs"

☞ Write all the documentation you must complete on a line that shows where the information must go.

My uncle has since passed away. His story is from around 1972. If I have a few facts wrong, please pardon me. He was the Managing Director of *a* fairly large company when he was admitted to hospital for an emergency procedure. There was no time to call meetings or to hand over work to his senior managers. The first day after his operation, he asked his wife to call the operations manager to come and see him in hospital. In the 70s mobile phones did not yet exist and there were no telephones by the beds of provincial hospitals in Cape Town. He had to wait for the manager to visit him in hospital in order to speak to him.

At this point, I must say that he was working an average of fourteen hours almost every weekday and most weekends. He was constantly tired, stressed and spent little time with his family; the usual story for most senior managers. After almost a full week the operations manager walked into the ward with a huge smile. By this time my uncle was extremely agitated and worried that the business was in some kind of chaos.

My uncle started questioning the manager about all the serious issues that he had been working on before being hospitalised. On every account there came a good answer. It became very clear very fast that the managers had evaluated what work needed to be done and had found someone amongst them who could handle that particular task. In some cases, they contracted outsiders, but they dealt with all the work that my uncle had thought only he could do. This was an eye opener for him, and a huge wake-up call.

By the time he was fit for work again, he had worked out a completely new style of management for himself and his staff. He did not do any work that was of a routine nature, nor did he touch a document that another manager reporting to him could handle. For the documents or situations that needed his attention, he would decide which manager must be trained to handle this kind of thing in the future. He never chaired any production, safety, problem-solving or any other routine meetings. He would be part of the meeting as a contributor and made his observer status clear by sitting away from the table in the corner (if he didn't do this, everybody kept looking at him for inputs and answers).

Afterwards he would have a one-on-one discussion with the person who had chaired the meeting to discuss technique, outcome of the meeting and so on. This way the chairman of the meeting grew in experience, knowledge and confidence. He did not slowly take back all the tasks. Soon he had almost no routine tasks to do and could concentrate on his actual job, which was to lead the company to greater profits, which he did with a team of willing and competent staff. He had time to walk around and observe. He started to learn the names of most of the workers, a few hundred in fact, and knew something personal about most of them. His method to get everybody pulling in the same direction was by influence, rather than by rules and instructions or pushing the cart by himself as he had done in the past. This worked very well. Much later I heard this style of management being coined: "Management by walking around".

What do we learn from this story?

- The people reporting to you want to do their work and are probably capable of doing so.

- You must empower your subordinates to do their work and support them in this.

- You can easily get very busy with a lot of non-KPA (key performance area) activities.

- You can fall into the activity trap (more about this later in this chapter).

- People are the most valuable asset in the organisation and a relationship with them will prove this to them.

- You are not irreplaceable; so do not act as if you are.

Performance reviews on KPA's:

You have agreed to produce a number of results in the areas of the business under your control. You will be measured against the agreed goals. Your staff has agreed to produce a number of results in the areas of the business under their control. They will be measured against those agreed goals. The purpose of a review is for the senior to evaluate the work of the junior and to make sure that the areas under his control are done to the agreed goals. I will repeat that for you in another way: the purpose of a review is for a manager to discuss the progress as per agreed goals and to help and assist the worker to achieve the goals with plans, advice and help.

The worker's area is inside the area of his manager on the same business map. The worker's performance influences his superior's performance and that of the business.

Keep the following in mind when you go into your review meeting:

1. Before you enter into the review meeting, you must have all the measurements for all the goals in your hand. If this is not available, postpone the meeting until it is. There is an example of KPA measurement in point 8 below.

2. Avoid any discussion other than about the KPAs.

3. The superior must give feedback on how the worker is doing based on facts alone. Do not discuss anything not based on facts. For example do not discuss the pile of scrap that looks "a bit high". Rather say: "The scrap rate is an unexcepted 0.8% above the alowed 0.5%". Salary adjustment will most likely be linked to the average mark of the KPA review. Hearsay can cost you points you cannot afford to lose.

4. The worker must be prepared to give reasons for the goals he did not achieve. Therefore it is necessary to keep records of machine breakdowns and other influences outside his control. He must also realise that poor performance plus a very good excuse still equals poor performance. Do not confuse effort with results. Nobody is paid to report for duty and make a huge effort; workers are paid to produce results. If the results are not there, then they are not there and the worker must acknowledge that he needs help. If the worker cannot reach one of the goals, it is most likely that there is a reason for it. You will know this before the meeting. Whether you are the worker or the manager, you must have a strategy ready when you enter the review meeting. There may be discussions about under-performance. Try to keep to

the facts. Later on in the chapter I will discuss the activity trap, a common reason for poor performance while working very hard. Use the information from there to motivate the assistance you need or will give. Almost all goals will be stretched goals. This means the goal will be difficult to reach. No point in having an easy goal, not for me anyway.

5. If a worker misses the mark and gets a rating of "poor" it means he either ignored the task or did not know how to achieve it. If it is the first case, he must study and apply the method to get out of the activity trap and pull up his socks. If he does not know how to perform the task in a way that gets the desired results he must ask for help from his manager. He must make sure the manager makes a commitment to help him with this problem by writing the help he will give him into his next goal and the target for the following evaluation period must depend on the help he receives. Then he needs to make sure the manager helps him with that task. There must be targets for them both. If not, he will just get a bad mark again and the area of the business will suffer. That is, after all why he is being managed. Apply this to your own staff in the same way.

6. You must realise that there will be new goals as soon as the present goal is achieved. This is great and you will grow as a manager while your worker will grow in his field of expertise. You must anticipate this and make sure that the goals are realistic and reachable. Go back to the KPAs above to read about this again.

7. Each key performance area must be evaluated with a mark or percentage. This percentage will most likely be linked to the salary adjustment at the end of the year. Make sure the performance review does not have the salary adjustment as its sole purpose. This way you will hear after one year that you have been doing a poor job from eleven months ago, or worse, you will tell your worker the above. The superior who does this knows that his worker struggled with something for all that time

without his having assisted him and stood by looking while the company missed its goals and lost money. This means that he had actually demonstrated to the worker what a poor manager he is and should most likely be disciplined.

8. You must be assertive (bold or forceful) in a polite way to make sure the mark allocated to an area is correct. It should be very simple to CALCULATE each point; never allow it to be estimated. For example; You must reduce the scrap rate below 3% from a present rate of 6% over the period of a year. In the first four months you manage the scrap rate from 6% to 5%., This means that you are on target to reach 3% or less in one year and must get three out of five for this area. If you did more than the target, you will get more than 3 out of 5 because 5 out of 5 means you did something over and above your target. Even if a 5% scrap rate is terrible, it was your goal and you achieved it. This is why every goal must be quantified so that your mark can be calculated. The worst thing that can happen to a person is his superior saying: "I feel you have not done what was expected of you since the pile of scrap outside is fairly high", and then giving you a one out of five where one is poor, two is below expectation, three is what was expected, four is more than expected and five is excellent.

> Poor performance plus a very good excuse still equals poor performance.

Needless to say I have made some performance review errors with those reporting to me because I did not have a good model from my seniors regarding KPAs and performance reviews, nor did I make a study of the subject like you are doing now. I have, however, never abused the performance review to give those reporting to me under-the-mark salary adjustments. The organisation you work for will have only so much money to adjust salaries and it has to be divided between all the workers. If your goals are not quantified, your review can go anywhere. You need a well-educated superior for this. If you have to, educate him while setting up the KPAs. The same applies to you as a manager. Make sure you use the KPA, or whatever performance measuring system is used in your organisation, in a correct and effective way.

Case study: The Company President:

Once again I do not want to mention this man's name. The story will remain the same. While working for a company whose main shareholder was an American **top** 500 company, I learned a few valuable lessons from a visit by the company President of our business. In his early thirties, he was very young for such a position. When he came to us for a board meeting in Botswana, the country just north west of South Africa, we all thought he would know little of the business since he had only been in this position for a few months. We were so wrong. After the introductions and pleasantries he wanted to see the factory. Needless to say, the factory was extremely clean. The factory had been stopped for two days before the visit to clean and prepare for his visit. This loss of production was not in the budget, that's for sure.

When he entered the factory area the plant was clean and producing at full speed. He looked around without comment and locked his eyes on a product sitting on rails off the conveyor. He enquired about it. Neither the Production nor the Operations Manager knew why it was there. They looked at the "product history" document attached to the product and saw that it was scrapped and the reason had been noted.

The Supervisor was called from the production machine and he confirmed this without looking at the document. All seemed well. Then the President asked what time the product had been made. With this knowledge he looked at the "two-hourly critical process variable log sheet" and the "change approval" document, a document where every setting change is noted with a signature from the Supervisor, to see if there were any changes made to the settings prior to the production of the scrap product. This check had not been done by either the Supervisor, the Production Manager or by the Operations Manger.

Sure enough, when they all looked at the documentation, they found that a critical component had been adjusted to a higher percentage just before the scrap was made. They also admitted that they never do this cross-reference check. The company president, with three months exposure to our business and very little or no production experience, basically told the Production Management, top to bottom, how to do their jobs and that they were there to produce product instead of reports and meetings, or whatever it was that kept them so busy. He knew about their core tasks' priorities better than they did.

What do we learn from this story?

- Never underestimate someone younger than yourself or assume anything about other people.

- It is easy to be so focused on the wrong things that you forget why you are there in the first place. In this case the management was so busy with reports and other non-core activities that they did not attend to their core task. More about this activity trap later on in this chapter.

- The factory must always be clean and free from rubbish or any unsafe condition. There is no point in misleading anybody by stopping the plant just to have a clean factory for a day or two. You must make a special effort on safety and cleaning all the time. The factory must be as clean as it can be every day.

What to do with your KPA?

We discussed KPAs, how to set them up and how to measure performance against them. Now here is what to do about KPAs.

Whatever result or output is expected of you, is expected of the section under your control or, better still, must be done by the people and processes you manage. There is no way you can produce the results for the areas under your control on your own. The people under your control will need to know what is expected of them in a very clear way, with clear goals; for example dates, times and quantities. There must be no misunderstanding about this. Their goals must be translated into tasks that can be measured per hour, per day, per week, per month and so on. Each task must be understood 100%. These tasks are normally linked to their particular skills and job descriptions.

The measurement of the key tasks is very important. The more often you do it, the sooner you will see if you or they are on or off track. If they are off the track; the effort and adjustment to get back is small, but if you wait too long between evaluations it will be much more difficult to get back onto track. Remember the catch phrase of the 80s:

> "You get what you measure".

Case study: My own KPA review meeting in 2004:

Every year we must get an adjustment in our salaries to combat inflation. Where I worked at the time they called it an increase and the review of **your** KPAs determined, **amongst other things, what "increase"** you would get.

All the KPAs I had had since the first one in 1985, including this one in 2004, were full of areas that could not be measured. As much as I tried to get them clear and measurable, I simply could not.

One of the KPAs was "Participation in the team". My manager told me that I had no idea about teamwork and gave me a very low mark. He could not provide proof and said it was how he saw it. I asked him when he first saw it and he said it was about from a year ago, making sure his point had some weight. The rest of the review was just as terrible and I left the office feeling cheated, bullied, angry and frustrated.

I decided to react by looking for a good book on the subject of teamwork. Just maybe this guy had a point and I did not want to give him the pleasure of telling me the same thing in my next review. From my research, I found that Dr. John Maxwell is an authority on leadership and team work. I bought his book. Before reading it I saw a website listed on the back cover. There was an assessment test for when you finished the book. I took the test immediately and scored an average 86%. I think I knew a lot about teamwork to get those marks, all by myself and from my own experience.

Categorise every task into A, B or C priorities:

You must motivate and influence your staff all the time. You must not do their work. People will try to get you to do their work and they will try to get you to make the decisions they were hired to make and let you take the responsibility so that if things go wrong, you are to blame. I have seen this happen at very high levels of management. Your job is to produce the results for the areas on the business map under your control. Managing your priorities into A, B or C will help you to focus on the right priorities and free up some of your time.

Every TASK you do can be sorted into three categories; namely: A, B or C.

☞ A relates to the core business of the organisation. A activities are the tasks that will directly result in something that can be invoiced and must be your most important KPAs.

☞ B is for the activities that indirectly relate to the core business of the organisation and must be your less important KPAs.

☞ C is for the activities that do not result in anything directly or indirectly related to the core business, but which still have to be done at one time or another. Make sure you understand that a C activity can be postponed in order to attend to an A or B activity. Better still, delegate the C activities if you can.

Examples related to a shoe factory:

A- activity: Discussing the production with an operator, making sure the machines are set for optimum production. Assist in fault finding to stop the sole being joined poorly to the shoe because of too little adhesive.

B- activity: Planning the tooling you need for next week's production run, order raw materials for night shift.

C- activity: Sorting out an invoice for adhesives delivered the previous month.

I will do it tomorrow:

People tend to say they will do things the next day. Sometimes this is true, but mostly they just do not plan their work well enough to what they set out to do. My answer to them is always the same:

> **TODAY is the TOMORROW of YESTERDAY.**

You are actually busy with the tomorrow of yesterday. All the work that you said "tomorrow" for must be done today plus the work of today.

The best way out of this cycle is to keep a record of your time and find out what it is that you really do every day.

Dealing with the activity trap:
There is so much to say about this that a book could be dedicated to the subject. This will, however, be enough to get you out of trouble and have you focusing on the right activities.

Senior as well as junior management can be extremely busy while not affecting the areas of the business they are appointed to affect or manage and they may not be delivering results to their full potential. In a previous case study, a man was in trouble for not doing his work while he was so busy that he had no time for lunch. As far as I know, there is only one sure way out of this problem and that is to take stock and take action. The only way to improve is to know what the situation is at present. Then you can formulate a plan to get to the desired outcome. I have done this more than once with fantastic results. It is something you do on your own, with or without the knowledge of your superior. Either way will give you results. It is an activity record.

To take stock you need to know what you are doing every minute of every day for at least one week. To do this is easy. Draw up a form with the following column headings: From; Activity; duration; category; comment. At the top you must make a space for your name and the date. The form must have about thirty rows.

<u>ToDo:</u>
Make five or more copies of this form. There is an example of such a form later in the chapter. From the minute you walk into your place of work the next day, start filling in the rows and columns. Do not cheat. The 'from' time is the time the previous row stopped. Apply a basic set of rules to categorise your activities into A, B or C as you go through the first day. If you are not sure in what category a specific activity falls, leave it blank to decide on later. Please note that training is an A activity because it influences the productivity of the worker

and addresses the number one reason for most non-productive issues, namely incompetence. You can expand on your activities to get more information. For example, AT can be training, an A activity in some cases. The sample below has two expansions: AT for training and CL for lost time or wasted time.

Write everything down. Do not fool yourself into thinking that you do not waste time. When last did you discuss a game or match with a colleague on a Monday, or have a cigarette outside the building? You can make more categories, as long as you can summarise how much time each category consumed after one week and work it out as a percentage of all the time spent. Keep it as simple as possible.

Make a note on the sheet of what you did not do that day. The next day you must attempt to do these tasks before 10am.

When you have all the data for at least five days, summarise it per category and sub–category, if you have used them. Evaluate the time you spent on each category and decide whether or not this contributed to the KPA or core business. If your factory produces shoes, did this time result in the production target being met or even exceeded? Do this for each activity.

<u>Ask yourself:</u>
☞ Must I do more of this activity to positively affect the goals in my KPAs?

☞ What will happen if I do not do this activity at all?

☞ Who else can do this activity?

☞ Can I delegate this activity? (Note that you can delegate upwards as well as downwards)

☞ Can I spread this activity to do smaller parts every day?

Then, when you have thought about all the activities and have come up with suggestions, go to your superior and discuss it with him. Get him involved to make sure you get the desired results. Ask him to assist where he can. This is very much in his interest as well as yours.

Refer to the sample that follows.

Record of daily activities				
Name: _John Maloe_			**Date:** _March 23 - Tuesday_	
From	**ACTIVITY**	**Duration**	**Category**	**Comment**
_8h00_	_Coffee, start PC, dress (coat and shoes)_	_15_	_CL_	
_8h15_	_Walk-about, production process_	_30_	_A_	_inspect, gather info from nightshift_
_8h45_	_Discuss production-previous shift_	_30_	_B_	_production target not met_
_9h15_	_Plan actions for today_	_21_	_A_	_Try and catch up over next 2 shifts_
_9h36_	_Phone calls and admin_	_6_	_C_	
_9h42_	_Fred in my office - discuss QC problem_	_16_	_C_	_not my problem_
_9h58_	_Tea and sandwich_	_6_	_CL_	
_10h04_	_Private calls (weekend plans :-)_	_6_	_CL_	
_10h10_	_Prepare for factory meeting_	_20_	_A_	
_10h30_	_Factory meeting_	_65_	_B_	_discuss and plans- QC, prod, maint_
_11h35_	_Adjust plan for today_	_25_	_A_	_new info - new plans_
_12h00_	_Discussions with production staff_	_18_	_A_	
_12h18_	_called to help on machine_	_6_	_A_	_setting not correct_
_12h24_	_Train operator_	_16_	_AT_	_explain how, why, test result, confirm_
_12h40_	_telephone calls_	_4_	_C_	_manager needs info_
_12h44_	_Go to town for lunch_	--------	-------	
_13h30_	_Meeting with maintenance_	_27_	_B_	_plan service on line 3_
_13h57_	_Walk-about, production process_	_33_	_A_	_inspect, assist, motivate etc_
_14h30_	_motivate, train 2 operators who are new_	_40_	_AT_	_explain how, why, test result, confirm_
_15h10_	_meeting - new production range_	_55_	_B_	_implement 2 weeks from now_
_16h05_	_write shift report_	_20_	_C_	
_16h25_	_Make sure materials for night shift are drawn_	_15_	_B_	
_16h35_	_call back 3 people_	_6_	_C_	
_16h41_	_Walk-about, production process_	_19_	_A_	_inspect, assist, motivate etc_
_17h00_	_Pack up and go_	_10_	_C_	
	DID NOT DO TODAY			
	adjust plan for today			
	Safety inspections for next week's meeting			

A = Directly related to KPA : _172_   **B = Indirectly related to KPA:** _192_   **C = Not related to KPA:** _62_

AT= Training: _56_   _509_

You can plot the information on a graph to give you an overview. The example below is for this one day. You must plot the whole week in one summary graph to give you a clear view of your activities.

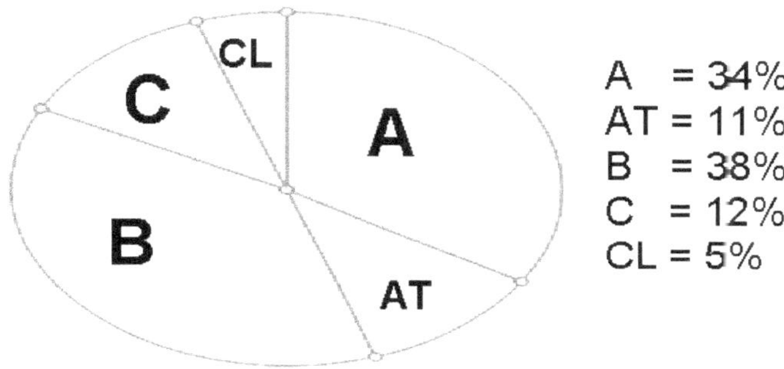

Interacting with your staff:
During a training session for a group of Managers and Supervisors I asked how many wheels a car has. This was a quiz we played as children and most of them knew it. The answers came as follows: four wheels on the ground, steering wheel and spare wheel. Then a technical person said fly wheel and later someone added the crown wheel. Next I asked which of these wheels was the most important. Many arguments followed, since the car needs all wheels to drive around. One man said it was the steering wheel, and he was right because the purpose of a car is to get from A to B. Without it the car would drive around aimlessly. Someone who had a bad experience with a flat tyre in a bad part of town argued for the spare wheel as it was the most important wheel on the car on that day at that instant. All very true.

Your job is to make sure that each member of your team knows he is important and contributes to the team. You must make sure that they know what is expected of them, measure their outcome and perform a review with them. The age-old saying: "You get what you measure" applies here. The one thing most managers fail to do is to follow up on the KPA reviews to train, educate and motivate the worker so that the next time the task is performed the result will improve.

More about this subject in the team building chapters.

The curved ball reality:
Think of your favourite sport. Now think of your favourite player. I'm sure this person performs very well. The reason they are on the team, or reached the top of that sport, is that they perform very well under the worst conditions. Take a baseball or cricket player for instance. They practice in the nets under relaxed conditions but, when they play a competitive game, they are under serious pressure from the opposition, from team members, from thousands of eyes fixed on every move they make and from the television broadcasts. The wind blows across the field and the pitcher or bowler delivers a curved ball. The player faces and handles the ball with style. This is why they are good, not because they perform well during practice sessions.

There are no excuses for poor performance. The player cannot give a good reason why he missed the ball. If his team loses it will be written down for all times to come. No excuses will be published in the history books or newspapers. If he does not perform well in match conditions he's out of the team.

In your work it is very much the same. You work in match conditions and you must deliver results regardless of the conditions. You cannot tell your manager that you received a curved ball and therefore you are not responsible for the results.

> If you miss a target, for whatever reason, the company misses the turnover, misses the income and misses the profit, while you did not miss your salary and the opposition scored a point.

An excuse is never a back door for poor performance. The better you can deal with the curve balls, the better manager you will become. You cannot get a good review on a poor job, even if you try your level best.

American President Harry Truman had a sign on his desk that said: "The buck stops here". Look it up on the internet if you want to make a copy for your desk to notify your colleagues that you are not passing on your responsibilities and definitely are not passing on blame.

Case study: Controlling spending:

This happened when computers and management software were well implemented, in the pipe factory where I worked in Botswana. Times were tough. Cash was scarce. Our MD told **us** that he had cancelled all signing powers for orders and that all orders and payments, regardless of value, must be approved and signed by him.

In this way he would manage all spending. -- -- WRONG!

This is what actually happened:

During the night shift, the continuous pipe winding machine had trouble advancing the pipe on a large diameter pipe. There could be several reasons for this, but the supervisor decided to replace the pushers, all twenty of them, with new ones. He dumped the old ones in the trash. The trash was cleared the next day before any person from management knew about the replaced parts. Later the next day the stores minimum-maximum system picked up that the stock level was below the minimum and it made an order for thirty-five new pushers. The value was very high. Only the MD could approve this spending, which he did after a meeting where he was very unhappy about the spending and where he also issued some threats.

What do we learn from this story?

- If you want to control costs, control the people who do the spending, in other words, control the consumption of raw materials, spare parts, overhead costs and so on.

- Once a resource is spent, used, or maybe wasted, it needs replacement, whether you like it or not.

- Having an hour meeting and issuing threats when you have to approve replacements in any case is pointless.

- The authorisation to replace spent resources was done by the person who authorises the use of items that need replacements. These are often people of low rank and no signing powers at all.

- In the story above, they should have called the MD in the night to ask his permission to use the new spare parts.

- To control spending, find the people using the resources and invest in their understanding of the business.

- If you change the way you approve spending, you change the map of the business and therefore the area under each person's responsibility. In our case the person did not know how his area was affected because if he had known he would have serviced the pushers with new springs or changed something else that affected the pipe forward motion.

What if your senior does not do his work?

The following case study or story is important to read and understand. It is not something that I am officially teaching you, but it is something that you have to understand because sooner or later it will happen to you, either as the worker or the manager. The story refers to your superior not doing his work and then dumping the responsibility on your shoulders. You will pay heavily if you fail and get absolutely no reward if you succeed. If this happens to you, you must discuss it with the relevant manger so that it does not happen often.

Case study: "Quickly do what I forgot":

When I was just twenty-two years old, in 1982, I worked for a technology company as an engineering student in their project department. When I arrived I saw a menthol applicator standing in the corner. After some weeks the department manager came rushing into the workshop with a wild expression in his eyes and fixed his gaze on me. He came over and asked if I could help him with a very important job that needed to be completed by Wednesday the following week. It was Friday then.

He explained that the menthol applicator unrolls a bobbin of paper, passes it through a spray-up applicator, where menthol is sprayed onto the paper and then it is rolled up again to make a new "menthol" bobbin. This menthol bobbin will then be used to wrap cigarettes. The cigarettes will be stored for a minimum period so that the menthol migrates into the tobacco.

The modification he wanted was to modify the machine to cut 15mm off one bobbin before rolling it onto the new bobbin. I had to remove the applicator and fix a cutting device in its place. I had three days. Luckily, I like challenges and thrive on pressure. This was what I signed up for.

On that same Friday I ran my first sample. I had a very sharp blade with an exhaust to suck away the off-cut. The first half of the bobbin had a good cut, but after that the blade was worn out and blunt and the edge of the paper became fuzzy. I was scratching my head, thinking how to solve this problem, when a senior technician and supervisor came to me and asked me what I thought I was doing. He was a month or so from retirement and a well respected person in the workshop. I told him that I am ...

"Yes I know" he interrupted me. *"You are making a fool out of yourself. Let me tell you something. This machine came here long before you. It arrived about two months ago and with it came an order to modify it to cut paper. The person who was to manage the project forgot all about it until they called him this morning to arrange for the collection of the completed project as per the original agreement. "The manager failed to do his work. He then found a willing sucker, that is you, to do something very quickly. Maybe you will succeed, and I think you will from what I see, but the job will not be fantastic, in fact it will look like a three-day job. Everybody at the factory knew the machine was here for two months. They will ask only one question: Who did this job? They will not ask how much time was given for the job, how big your budget was or any other question. My advice to you is the following:*

"This is a two-months job, so take all the time you need and do it correctly. If the factory asks for it and it cannot be delivered, the manager will be in trouble, not you. It is, after all, his mistake.

"Make a proper study of the requirements. Go to the technical office and ask them if there are any other paper cutting devices already employed in our technology.

"Look at the present cutting technology and design a few changes so it will work on this applicator machine.

I followed his advice and made a fantastic cutting machine. The original exhaust turned out to be the best I could make. All the parts were treated and painted, packed properly and labelled. It was a job to be proud of. The whole job took me four weeks. After another few weeks, when I'd left to return to my studies, the modified applicator was still in the corner, waiting to be collected.

What do we learn from this story?:

- Apparently I learned little from that experience because I have since then, as a senior person, fallen for the same trick several times, just because I like a challenge so much. Sales people made ridiculous promises and I had to fulfil them. Most of what I did came out well, but some of it cost me dearly. I did, however, come to me senses a few times and rejected the invitation to make an idiot of myself.

- You can learn from this. I do not say refuse to help your boss when he is in trouble, but if he makes a habit of it you will have to draw a line somewhere.

- If you are the manager who forgot the thing and now expect the team to work through weekends, during nights and to bend over backwards to get you out of trouble, I suggest that you tell them you screwed up and needs help and if the effort is a failure, DO NOT LET THEM TAKE THE BLAME.

Appointing workers:

The people who do the work you must manage are either already there or must be appointed. As the years pass you will eventually appoint new workers.

In the next chapter we will deal with the FAST principle (faithful, available, submissive and teachable). You must keep this in mind when you look for new staff. You must know exactly what you want. Do at least the following.

Draw up a requirement:

☞ What must the worker do?

☞ What minimum qualifications must he have?

☞ What is the minimum experience the worker must have?

☞ If his experience is not exactly relevant, who will train the worker?

☞ If he must be trained, how much will it cost?

☞ If we train the worker, must we fix the employment contract with a period for the worker to "work back" the investment?

☞ What will the salary range be?

☞ Work in shifts, weekends, regular 9-5 etc?

☞ To whom must the person report?

☞ When must the worker start?

☞ Is it a new position or a replacement?

☞ If the worker will not report to yourself, get the new worker's supervisor involved in the setting up the requirements.

☞ How much may you spend on advertising?

☞ Do you use an agent (they charge a fee)?

☞ In chapter 7 we deal with communication styles. If possible, read that chapter before you make your final list of requirements.

Plan the recruitment:

If the company has an HR (Human resources) department you can work closely with them. Let them do the recruitment from here on. If not, use an agency to help you. If you must do it yourself, ask for help from the senior managers who have experience and plan every step of the process that is listed below. Even if somebody else does it, stay involved.

Advertise:

A job advert is news to those who are looking for a new job. Every profession reads different newspapers, looks at different websites, etc. Some media are common to all, for example job-related sites (and there you will find categories). Decide where to advertise. Maybe you will use an agent and they will do all of this.

Interview:

- Prepare for the interview.
- Know what you want to ask and what answers you need to hear in order to decide if a candidate is the right fit for the work.
- Ask direct questions regarding aspects that are important to you, for example: drinking habits, arrival on time, respect for authority, absenteeism, etc.

After the interviews:

Compare notes against the requirement. Do not let superficial things dictate your decision-making process.

Once you have a candidate:

- Decide on the offer to make him;
- judge how much training he will need before he will be making a 100% contribution;
- ascertain when he should start;
- have a plan for if he rejects the offer,
- choose who the second choice is (and start from the top of the list with him.)
- advertise again and advertise wider (in other cities or countries) if you do not get a good candidate.

Cross references:

Call the people the person lists as references. You may even ask the reference for another name to call and in doing this rule out the "prepped" references. Ask questions that will help you determine important characteristics about the person, for example: drinking habits, arrival on time, respect for authority, absenteeism, etc. Basically, cross reference what the person has said in the interview.

<u>Pitfalls when appointing workers:</u>
☞ Over qualification: a bored worker is a dangerous condition and must be avoided. Apply a worker in the top half of his ability and qualifications.

☞ Family: All is well if all goes well, but sooner than later you will need to apply discipline, or withhold favours to treat all workers equally and having family-employees makes this task nearly impossible.

☞ Friends: The same goes for friends as for family members above.

☞ "Favours": If you employ somebody because you owe him (or whoever) a favour, it will not work out. People must be employed because you need the service they provide. If not, they lose dignity, you get in trouble with other workers who are there to work and so on.

☞ "The only one who responded": If you need a worker and have only one respondent, make sure that the worker meets at least 70% (for example) of the requirements. If not, you'll end up doing the work yourself, anyway. Rather change the requirements, the strategy or whatever and keep looking because you will also do the person who is in the wrong job an injustice.

☞ Agents: Sometimes they disregard all you ask of them and pass on every candidate they can find without pre-interviews or selection and without regard to your requirements. When you make the order with the agent, make sure they know what to do for you.

<u>Starting with the new worker:</u>
The first day in the workers career with you is very important. Help him to establish himself.

Teach or train the worker to do the specific tasks that are specific to your company.

Teach the worker your industry to familiarise him with the environment. This is called induction training.

Checks to make sure you have the benefit of this chapter:

	Yes	No
I know what my responsibilities are and I have a copy of the Key Performance Areas:	☐	☐
I have agreed to the targets and goals for each area:	☐	☐
I have a plan of how to achieve each goal:	☐	☐
I have an assistance agreement with my superior if I realise that I am struggling with any of the goals in my areas:	☐	☐
I have filled out an activity form for at least five consecutive days:	☐	☐
I have summarized the A, B and C activities and discussed the results with my superior to ask his assistance with a plan of action:	☐	☐
I am getting the business results that relate to my KPAs:	☐	☐
I will study and analyse the business results and will make plans and actions to improve:	☐	☐
I will prepare for my next review meeting:	☐	☐
I will have respect for my staff and make everyone feel important and valuable:	☐	☐
I understand the curved ball theory:	☐	☐
When I appoint a person, I will do my best to get the right person for the job and follow all the correct steps to appoint him:	☐	☐

4

Your staff's responsibilities

As a manager, your job is to make sure you manage your staff and the work they do in order to achieve predetermined and agreed products, outputs or specific results.

Who are your staff? What can they do? Are they the right people to get the results expected from you? If they are FAST, they can be the right people to start with, to teach and to train, to believe in, to trust, to take responsibility and to deliver.

What is a FAST person?

Faithful – They must have faith in the product or service the company provides. They must believe you can manage the work, the process and themselves. They must be faithful, in a sense of loyalty, to the team.

Available – They must report for duty and be available for extra work if there is a peak to deal with. Their work must be a priority to them.

Submissive – They must submit to your authority over them. The must submit to the company rules and regulations and respect others.

Teachable – They must be able to listen and evaluate a new instruction or method and have the ability to learn something new, regardless of the fact that they may have been doing it another way for many years.

Some bad advice:

A person once gave the following advice to a newlywed husband: he told him that, as soon as they got back from honeymoon, he should offer to wash the dishes and then break a few plates and glasses. His wife would kindly instruct him never to wash any dishes again. I do not believe any woman will be so stupid as to fall for such a trick, yet I have seen many managers do the work of their staff late into the night because they think they can do it better without the worker having to first make a disaster of the job. Any worker will always be happy with this arrangement.

Let us look at "responsibility"

From www.businessdictionary.com, the definition of responsibility is: *"Duty or obligation to satisfactorily perform or complete a task (assigned by someone, or created by one's own promise or circumstances) that one must fulfil, and which has a consequent penalty for failure".*

If I say, for example, that my staff is responsible it means that I know they will make it their business to know what I expect of them, then do it right and that I will be able to predict their response to my instructions.

Your staff must understand that they have a task to perform. If they cannot do it they must ask for help, not sit and wait for you to do the job for them. Your job is to help them do the task by explaining, showing, observing, questioning, explaining again, observing, questioning, explaining, and observing and so on until they can do it. At no point are you to take over the task and finish it.

> Your staff must understand the following formula very clearly:
>
> **A poor job + a very good excuse = a poor job**

Make sure your staff is responsible for what you expect of them. You will have to demand results even if you know they cannot give them. If they cannot do it, they must ask you for help or ask another person for help and still produce the results you expect of them. During this time, train and guide them closely while you help them. By helping them, you must not take over their job or relieve them of their responsibilities.

Make sure they know what you expect of them. Do this all the time and they will start being responsible to the point where you can focus your efforts elsewhere and they can work on their own.

Case study: Call outs at night for the Maintenance Manager:

Many years ago a friend of mine arrived at a factory as the new Engineering Manager. Almost from the first day he was called out in the night **to** assist either the electrician or mechanical artisan with finding faults and repairing machines that broke down. None of the problems were really out of the ordinary or extremely complex and it bothered him that an artisan needed help with basic work. After about the fourth call-out he asked the artisan to report to his office the next morning with an original copy of his qualifications for a meeting to establish whether or not he was qualified to do this job. The artisan was then re-interviewed for the job and his references re-checked. These proved to be in order, which meant he was just not doing his work. He went through a disciplinary procedure for not performing his basic tasks After that there were no more call-outs for my friend and breakdowns were repaired a lot faster. This proves that the other artisans realised that they should do the job for which they were hired, or get into trouble. I learned from this and did exactly the same thing where I was the maintenance manager. In my case, I had two disciplinary hearings for people not doing their work and not taking up their responsibilities, after which I was no longer called out during the night for nonsense.

What do we learn from this story?:

- Never pass your responsibility upwards. If you have trouble doing your job ask for help, but keep the responsibility.

- Never abuse a person's willingness to help you.

- Never waste other people's time.

- Respect other people's time away from work.

- If you do the same stupid thing several times in succession you will be caught and may get into trouble.

Managing disappointment:

A definition I have found over the years for disappointment is:

> "Disappointment is the difference between what you expected and what you got".

If your workers know what you expect from them they are less likely to disappoint you.

You must tell your staff it is their duty to renegotiate your expectations if they realise they are going to miss your expectations. Then, and only then, are you in control again and you can either adapt what you expect to what they can do, or you can help them or give them more resources to reach the original goal.

You can stop being disappointed by your staff.

How do you manage people to take up their responsibilities?
Ask yourself: How would I like to be managed? Ask the staff member reporting to you how he would like to managed. It may sound very stupid to ask such a question, but it is not if you stick to the subject of communication and motivation. Each person responds to instructions in a different way. You can try to accommodate the staff as far as possible.

Use the following guidelines to manage your staff with regards to their responsibility:

- ☞ Do daily checks to monitor the worker. If the worker has a clear understanding of the tasks you can stretch the checks to weekly or even monthly.
- ☞ The instruction must be in a written format, understood and signed by both him and you.

☞ If the staff member works on a machine or process there must be a Standard Operating Procedure for him to follow. Test the knowledge of the staff member by giving a written test. Use the results to train and retrain until the procedure is understood 100%.

☞ Be visible and attend to the staff as much as you can. If you sit in a remote office, nothing will happen.

☞ Be firm and discipline any wrong behaviour from day one: For e.g. late coming, lying, cheating, etc.

☞ Do not befriend your staff. You are in a leadership position and clear guidelines for the staff are necessary to cultivate respect. It may help if your staff addresses you in a formal way.

☞ Do not be overly authoritarian, state what you expect, keep to your end of the agreement.

☞ Always be respectful.

☞ You are all there to do a job, not for social reasons.

☞ Work must be you first concern and priority. You can build a relationship with the staff in the lunch hour, inside the canteen.

☞ Always have open channels of communication. We can all learn from one another.

☞ Expect the best and teach the correct response if you do not get it.

☞ Expect of them what they agreed to as a goal and deal with shortfalls in a firm and formal manner. Help and train the person if you have to.

☞ Reward outstanding results and behaviour. Good work is a prerequisite for a standard pay cheque at the end of the month.

☞ Acknowledgement is a good reward, use it to motivate and inspire your staff.

☞ Address dishonesty, criminal activity and negligence immediately in a formal manner. There is a chapter later in this book that is dedicated to legal procedures that you can use as a guideline.

☞ Be strict with favours. It is better to have a rule of no favours.

☞ Be careful if you befriend your staff socially. This will make it extremely difficult to keep discipline if you are not able the separate work from social relationships.

☞ Avoid romantic relationships in your team. If this happens, ask for a transfer for one of them.

☞ Study the chapters on team-building in a later chapter where there are a lot more tips on the subject.

> Your staff has only one purpose: WORK.
> Make sure they do it and do it well.

Work and salary: My friend's viewpoint:

A friend of mine who managed a printing business for many years asked me some time ago what a person must do to get a good salary. My answer: A good job.

"You are wrong, Piet, a good job is what people are hired to do as an absolute minimum. A good job will get a person an average salary. This is the "entry level". A better than good job will get a person a better than average salary. A fantastic job will get a person an excellent salary."

Do you agree with the above? Then tell your staff, but only if it will be possible for you to actually pay the top performers more than the *average* rest and if you have a solid KPA system in place to manage work performance. As for yourself, do a better than good job anyway because the reward will follow sooner rather than later.

"Stop Jobs"

Believe it or not, there are many workers standing around doing nothing. You will miss your targets if you do not address this issue. This can and will happen in your department. The reasons for it can be:

- Waiting for raw material.
- Waiting for the machine to be repaired.
- Waiting for a tea break or end of shift (a job might take longer than the time left to the break).
- There is no documentation.
- Waiting for further instructions.
- Cannot do anything because a key person is absent.

The way to deal with this is to have a list of tasks ready for them to do if the regular task cannot be performed for whatever reason. Never give only one task at a time. Give multiple tasks and make sure most of the tasks can be done with less than the full team. As soon as something prevents them from doing their normal work they, even if it is one person, must revert to the list of tasks or Stop Jobs. One task that must definitely appear on the list is cleaning and housekeeping. It is a proven fact that if the alternative tasks are not so nice to do the workers will apply special effort and initiatives to keep doing the regular job and produce the results that meet the target. This way you can meet your target and if something really prevents the staff from performing their normal jobs you have the benefit of other completed tasks, even if it was cleaning. You will have to monitor the log sheets and reports carefully and be firm with the staff if they neglected to do a "Stop Job" when something prevented them from doing their normal work.

Understand the staff's abilities:

The staff you are managing may be illiterate, highly educated or anywhere in-between. This will determine the relationship and management style you must apply and the responsibility you can expect from each of them. You must determine how much you have to instruct and how much you must check on each person. Do not frustrate your staff by under-estimating their abilities. Communicate to them at their own level.

The weakest link in a chain determines the strength of the chain. If you can identify this person you can pay more attention and give more help so that this person is no longer the weakest link and the "chain" can take the full load.

A group moves at the pace of the slowest person. There can be many reasons a person is slowing down a group. Help to "carry" this person so that the goal of the group is reached. Extra training and help will get this person up to speed. If he simply cannot "speed up", find another job for him in the company or let him go so that you can appoint the right person.

Case study: My son Bryan, the Engineering student:

From the time he could walk, my son Bryan was always following me whenever I walked into the garage (workshop at home) and helped whenever I would allow it. Now he studies Engineering and is as keen to help and work as always. A few years ago we designed and build a pipe winder at my work. We were not enough people to handle all the testing ourselves and I hired extra help. Bryan was the ideal helper and fortunately he had holidays.

- He constantly looked around to see who needs help or who struggled and told me if a task is completed.

- He asked questions to make sure he does the work right

- He wanted to learn and he did.

- He took responsibility for any task I gave him.

- He handled my complaints if things went wrong. (development will always have unforseen problems and set-backs)

- He did not mind to get very dirty with resin and other raw materials.

- He did any job, from grinding, mixing resin, collect goods in the city or whatever I threw at him.

- He was always on time and ready for work, even late into the evening.

> Never do your best - do it RIGHT.

Checks to make sure you have the benefit of this chapter:

I do not and will not take over any tasks from my staff, even if they struggle with them: ☐ ☐

I understand the concept of responsibility: ☐ ☐

I made a list of "stop jobs" and handed it to the staff: ☐ ☐

I have worked out the level of responsibility for my staff and I have decided how much control each member should have: ☐ ☐

Each member of my staff has a clear knowledge of what is expected of him. ☐ ☐

 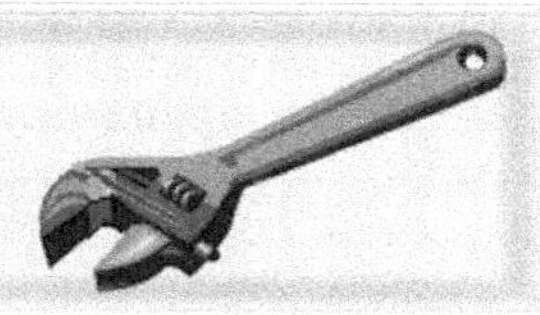

Management tools

Whatever you do, you will need tools. As a manager you must have access to many tools. I will do my best to list as many as possible. For fist-time and junior managers, supervisors and such people, this chapter will deal with the "new" tools or skills they will need. It is as practical as I can make it simply because a "tool" is something like a book, software or a service you can use or apply. If you are a well-established manager you can make sure that you have these basic tools and fine-tune them.

Your old tools:

You obviously had a good set of tools or skills to do your previous job if you were promoted into management. You may have to lay down some or all of those tools if you want to be a good manager. It is possible that the people you manage need those tools now.

Some people are in management positions based on their qualifications or other shortcuts and therefore did not get there through the "ranks" and as a result do not have any old "tools". For them it will be easier to take up the new tools.

Remember the story discussed in chapter 3, about the supervisor who was promoted and got into trouble for not doing his new job properly? He not only kept his old tools, but kept on using his old tools and skills and that got him into trouble.

You old tools can be:

☞ A toolbox with spanners, hammers etc.

☞ A computer with specific software.

☞ Documentation.

☞ Electronic equipment.

☞ Specific skills and knowledge or anything to perform your previous task.

Maybe you are straight from your studies and have no experience yet and all this is new to you. If so, welcome!

Your new tools:

Regardless of who and what you manage, you need to get the right tools. If it is your first time in a management position the tools may be new.

If you manage people, you must get them to do the work. Your tools can be anything from a diary to a specific skill as long as they help you to reach the targets set out in your KPAs. Your tools can be any or all of the tools listed below and some not listed. Study each tool carefully to see if it will help you:

⚊◆ Tool 1: Diary and planner

You need to plan your day, week, month and year. There are meetings to attend, dates to remember and so on. You must make sure you know these dates and write them into the diary. Study the diary every night for the next few days to make sure you are prepared for what is planned. You can also use the diary to keep other information. Some diaries have loose pages for notes and so on. Keep a ToDo list and update it daily. Make the list visible on the "day" pages.

Remember to:

> Plan your work – then work your plan.

✎ Tool 2: Taking notes

As a manager, you will "juggle many balls". This means you will do several tasks at the same time. Information will reach you almost non-stop and you will have to remember an awful lot. You must get into the habit of noting down the information that needs follow up or further processing. To do this there are a few methods for taking notes.

☞ A small pocket book that fits into your shirt pocket. Carry it with a pen and use it while not at your desk to make notes. Then deal with the pocket book notes when you get back to your desk. This could be a phone call to somebody, following up on administration, transferring the note to the ToDo list and much more.

☞ Smart phones or other electronic devices can take notes just as easily.

☞ A large A4 notebook that you must keep on your desk. If your diary is large enough you can allocate a portion of each day's page for this. Use this book to scribble and make notes while you speak on the phone, when you write down numbers, when you speak to somebody and note actions down. Draw a line under each day and make sure you write the date. Also make sure you deal with each note before the day is out and write the things you need to follow up in the ToDo list of the next day. Never scribble on the desk pad or loose papers that will be blown away by the wind. Keep these books for lookup purposes later on. You can do this on an electronic device, but I have found that it is not the same as a book.

☞ When looking for something you wrote down, your brain will remember the side of the page, top or bottom, pen colour and many other things. It is more difficult to do this back checking on electronic device.

�🔧 Tool 3: Databases

Records and data are very valuable management tools. This can be as simple as asking someone who has worked in your area for a few years what happened in the past. You need to know all you can about the past and apply the data to give you trends, to find reasons for highs and lows and so on. This can prevent you from repeating mistakes and you can build on and improve on past successes.

There must be a formal record-keeping system. Make sure you know what records are kept and ask the manager of that area to include records you need to keep. Also ask for outputs from the data you need that is collected at specific times like month-ends. This information must be utilised to plan and improve on the performance of that month.

�🔧 Tool 4: Internet and libraries

Knowledge and information resources should be within reach of anybody in a management position. If you are not in the habit of reading and researching your area of work you can start today. Most big towns have libraries with an array of books on almost every subject. The staff in the business section will help you find the right book. Some libraries have computers that are connected to the internet.

The internet is all about information, or rather that is how it started. A lot of money is made on the internet by selling information, but some of it is free. Search engines search web pages twenty-four hours a day and build databases of key words. When you ask it to search for a word or phrase it will consult the database and show you the link to each document where the words you searched for appear. Here are some tips for working with search engines:

☞ One-word searches deliver huge numbers of results and should be avoided.

☞ Some words can have more than one meaning and the search results might shock you. If this happens you do not have to click on any of those links.

☞ If you want to search for two or more words and they must be in the same document put a plus sign in front of each word, for example: +management +tools.

☞ If you want a phrase searched, put it in "quotes just like I'm doing now". You can search phrases and words for the same document if you want to.

☞ Refine your search to include more key words until you get what you need.

☞ Do not search subjects not related to your work on your work computer. This will get you into serious trouble. Please be aware that some sites have no moral values or ethics and will record your addresses and other information and bombard you with junk or, worse, hack your server to steal information.

☞ Do not give your email address to any website unless it is absolutely necessary. This policy will reduce junk mail.

☞ Email is part of what the internet offers. There is a tool dedicated to this topic. Please read it.

☞ If your company has an internet policy, make sure you study it before using the internet.

Example: internet information:

I recently upgraded the software of my phone only to find that whatever I knew about it does not apply any more. I could not find a way to set the notification sound for incoming email. After ten minutes of searching on the phone I entered the following line in the search engine: "Blackberry sound incoming email". This gave me the answer in less than a minute. If you are not in the habit of asking for information on the internet you must try it as soon as possible. It will save you a lot of time.

➤ Tool 5: Qualifications

One of the most powerful tools in your box is your qualifications. Certainly there are arguments that theoretical qualifications don't prepare you to do the job, but do not believe it for a second. The fact is that qualifications are important as they give you the foundation you need for a more senior job or position. In the process of getting a higher qualification you will have expanded and developed your thinking, reasoning powers and you as a person. Some positions need minimum qualifications by law. If you missed the opportunity to study earlier on in your life you can start now. There are many distance learning institutes waiting to teach you. Most companies will assist their loyal workers with studies. I know of a seventy-two-year-old grandmother who studied and received a doctorate in business.

Do not think that your initial qualification is enough to equip you for life. Maybe it is, most likely not. Get into the habit of searching the internet for new ideas and developments in your field. Enrol for another qualification if you can. To quote one example, I did an extra qualification when I was in my early thirties. I enrolled for a business development course at the Business school of the University of Stellenbosch to help me find my feet in the area of Management. We had small children at the time and it took as much from my wife as from me to do this course. In the end, though, it was worth all the hard work, late nights and little sleep.

My wife, for example, could no longer practice Physiotherapy, her initial qualification, and studied to be a preschool teacher. After a few years she studied in the evening program of the university to qualify herself as a high-school teacher, just to broaden her qualifications, widen her opportunities and to enjoy the bigger children.

What is your excuse?

Tool 6: A mentor

I was fortunate to have parents with experiences in many areas of life who gave me lots of advice. Unfortunately, my father died when I was just twenty-one years old and with it I lost my mentor. Luckily I had older friends and family. I have also sought lots of advice from other business people. Never think you can tackle complex problems on your own if you are not experienced. Later on, with many years of experience, you will be able to do so, as well as help others. Find somebody with experience and bounce some ideas around before you try them out in your work. Family members, friends of your parents and so on are usually willing.

Tool 7: Reports

You need to report exactly what happens within the area of the business under your control. You must report at preset intervals and must give a summary of statistics, trends, highlights, low points and so on, to reflect the performance of your team. There are many reasons for a report, which must be centred around how many of the agreed goals you and your team accomplished. Your manager has to know the results of the area under his control and must report on it as well. Your manager must, in turn, influence and manage the results by assisting you with ideas, help and advice and must make the necessary resources available to help you if you did not reach the desired results.

Make sure you know what kinds of reports are expected and at what times. You must gather the information you need to make the reports on time.

Needless to say, the report must look good. Use the same font throughout, use company stationary and use a standard form if your company has it. Use the spell checker to correct mistakes.

> Do not spend more time and effort writing the report than you do managing and influencing the results. Doing so would be like the proverbial "arranging the deck chairs of the Titanic".

Tool 8: Meetings

I have seen and experienced almost every type of meeting. There are formal boardroom meetings; stand up meetings, passage meetings and anything in-between. The effectiveness is rarely determined by the method of the meeting but rather by the agenda and the way the agenda is managed. Do not blindly copy the way your supervisor conducts his meetings. Evaluate his meetings, extract good methods and then make it your own. Think carefully about what you want out of the meeting and plan the agenda carefully.

Points to remember when you plan a meeting:

- Allocate time that you think is enough to spend on each topic and stick to it. If a subject takes longer than the allocated time, you can call a separate meeting for it with the relevant people present and report back at the next meeting or just add the outcome to the minutes of the meeting.

- Establish some ground rules and stick to them as far as possible.

- Keep to the time allocated for the meeting.

- Keep minutes or a record of what must be done from the discussions. Do not write essays, but note down what must be done by whom and by when. Number each item consecutively. Delete what has been done. This numbering system will highlight the numbers that are old and is also a visible measurement of the work that has been done and progress that has been made.

- Ask if somebody wants to add something to the agenda; do it before the meeting, otherwise your staff will come unprepared, sit there and dream up a lot of items to discuss without being prepared and also without you having been able to prepare. If a matter arises during the meeting and it is not really very urgent, tell the person it will be added to the next meeting's agenda or make a separate meeting for it. This will result in preparation for the meetings.

Do not fall into the trap so many managers before you have fallen into. This is called a "history trap" where people give a report of what happened yesterday and blame others for what did not happen yesterday. Try your best to concentrate on what must be done today to affect the results in your area for tomorrow. After all, whatever is discussed about yesterday's production and the reasons for not making it is pure entertainment and history. Nobody can change the past. Let all your staff discuss the challenges facing them over the next period of time. What is done is done and no amount of discussion on the past can change it. The chances are almost 100% that the discussions of the past will end up as a mud-throwing and blaming party. If production results of the previous day must be reported, put it on a board before the meeting. The targets and achievements must be marked clearly for all to see. This way you do not have to waste time talking about it. You can then talk about what to do today and beyond to make sure they improve on the expected results. You need to focus the discussions on the plans and actions for each person so that the rest of today and tomorrow will be productive. The people in the meeting can then contribute with plans and ideas and you will have the benefit of the experience and knowledge of the group to influence tomorrow's results.

Do not use the meeting to manage your staff. Meet with each member of staff responsible for something at his place of work on a daily basis and ask everything you need to know, then help by giving advice and make plans together. Your staff deserves to go to a meeting without their time being wasted by watching you do your work. This will be boring for them and they may fall asleep, as I have done a few times in meetings that went on and on and on and on about subjects that were not related to me or that I had no interest in.

Tool 9: Motivational skills

If you are motivated, your staff should be as motivated as you are. I can assure you that there will be times when you struggle with this. Learn to keep your head up and focus on what is good and what can be done positively in the next hour, the next day or the next week. Never start talking with other unmotivated people for this will pull you down into a depression. Seek the company of positive and motivated people all the time and their nature will rub off on you.

To motivate your staff to be disciplined, loyal and hard working you can do the following:

☞ Respect them.

☞ Communicate the team goals.

☞ Communicate the team results.

☞ Never talk them down or belittle them.

☞ Always make time to discuss their problems and help where you can or arrange for help if you cannot provide it yourself.

☞ Give feedback on performance to the team and individuals.

☞ Develop them as a team and as individuals.

☞ Make sure they are paid in relation to their work and do not exploit them.

☞ Encourage rather than demand.

☞ Be firm about the do's and don'ts to create a secure environment.

☞ Understand the culture of your staff and accommodate differences.

☞ Reward extra work with something useful other than money.

☞ Create a safe environment.

☞ Be honest.

☞ Be consistent.

Tool 10: Management skills

This tool is huge. You can study it forever without knowing it all. This page does not represent the whole book, it highlights a few points. Here are some important aspects of management you must understand and implement as fast as possible:

☞ Understand financial reports and understand the finances that make a business tick over.

☞ Understand the various roles of other departments like finance, sales, engineering, production, human resources, legal department and others.

☞ Study and understand as much as you can about human science in order to appreciate different people in your team (there is a chapter on this in this book).

☞ Study and understand the legal side of your business. What laws govern your trade?

☞ Make a list of experts that you can ask for advice on various subjects.

☞ Realise that even the biggest house was built brick by brick. This means that each aspect of management can be broken down into understandable and do-able pieces that are not as difficult to deal with as the whole.

You have to get exposure to management other than through the position you presently occupy. A good way to get experience is to get involved in committees. Here you will work with a broad spectrum of people in your organisation and you will see them work and learn from them and get to know them. It is also a good place to add value and get noticed.

One way to get experience in a higher management position is to join a volunteer organisation. This can be anything from neighbourhood forums, clubs, school governing bodies, rescue institutes, Churches and many more. There you will work with others who will expose you to management. You will get involved and exchange ideas with all sorts of experts from all sorts of industries. Soon you will find yourself getting valuable experience in all areas of management. Very importantly, you will work in an environment where you will not be judged based on your rank or position at work. You must appreciate that nobody gets paid in these organisations and for this reason the motivation, persuasion and management methods must be very good because the people cannot be persuaded with money rewards and they are not obliged to take orders like in an organisation where they are paid. The leaders are mostly very good at managing people and you can learn a lot from them. I have been doing exactly this and even received formal management training through the organisation I served as a volunteer.

Case study: Getting experience

I would like to relate a true story to motivate you with regards to getting experience. In 1995 a colleague of mine complained that he was not getting *a* fair deal. He had recently qualified as an Engineering Technician after three years of studies and the company did not adjust his salary from student to Shift Supervisor, the job he was doing at the time. That particular industry went through a very bad recession and all promotions were stopped indefinitely. On top of everything, he was asked to take on extra responsibilities. He was discouraged and angry.

My advice was the advice I received from one of my mentors a few years earlier. I asked him what he was worth and what his salary was. The difference was the investment he made every month to "pay" for experience. At that stage his plan was to tell management that he was not prepared to do all the work they expected of him for the money they paid. I helped him to realise that he must make sure he got value for his investment. He must also keep a record of his investment and what experience he gets for it. He must then find a buyer for all the experience he bought with "non salary". He picked up on this idea so much that he volunteered for even more responsibilities to get experience in the areas he lacked. About eight months later he started looking for new employment to sell the experience he had "bought" with the shortfall in his salary because the present company was not interested or able to buy it from him. He landed a fantastic job with a very good salary. After this job interview he was very excited when he told me how they questioned him on the areas of quality management, one of the responsibilities he had volunteered for to get more experience.

⚙ <u>Tool 11: Teaching</u>

The results of the department or section you manage are your number one objective. To achieve the results every person must do his work well. Unfortunately, people get sick, get into accidents, pass away or move on. There is nothing we can do about it. When this happens, somebody else must do that person's work with a high degree of efficiency, even if it is your own work. You must make sure this is possible by teaching your staff.

A friend and mentor gave me the following advice as a young man: "If you want to make progress in your work and in life, duplicate yourself in others and work yourself out of a job". Apart from that advice, my late father always taught me how to do everything he did. Later I realised he was doing exactly what my friend had told me to do. Today I know the value of it more than ever before. You must learn to do the following to be a successful teacher:

☞ Take stock of the skills and knowledge of your staff.

☞ Draw up a training program to give the skills and knowledge to those who need it by either teaching them yourself or hiring somebody else to teach them.

☞ Find written material like manuals, books, explanations on the topic and present it to the members of staff who need it.

☞ Use the companies training budget to buy training material and courses.

☞ Hand down your knowledge and skills to individuals.

☞ Ask others with specific skills to teach your staff.

☞ Make use of suppliers to teach you and your staff about their goods and technology.

☞ Attend trade shows relevant to your industry and brief your staff on what you have seen and learned to keep them enthusiastic and up to date. If possible, take one of your best performing workers with you.

☞ Use those people in the team with more knowledge and experience to teach the others.

☞ Cross-train your staff. Make sure you move the people around so that every task is known to at least two people. Do not do this in a secret way, but make sure it is a formal documented process with training, tests, assistance, evaluation and recognition. This goes for your own job as well. While you may like to think that only you can do your work, if you do you are a fool. This is a harsh statement, but very true. The reality is that if you fall ill for a short period, or you must travel, someone must make sure the work is done to the expected result. Nobody will really take control of your position in a few days with such effectiveness that you will be redundant unless you are not doing your job well.

Teaching does not stop at telling somebody how to perform a specific task. It includes developing that person. You will soon see who on your team can be trusted with decision-making and responsibility. Use them and mentor them without discouraging them. If they make decisions, comment truthfully.

> Never tell your staff that six is better than their half a dozen just for the sake of correcting them and highlighting your own superiority.

This will wear them down. It happened to me for many years. Nothing I did found approval the first time. There was always something meaningless to change. You must never do this. To break somebody down will result in uncertainty and your staff will have to check with you before they make any decision. Be mature and trust your staff. Allow them to see the results of their decisions. They will make better decisions each time.

To illustrate a point I would like to tell you how I helped my younger brother with his mathematics problem. He was about fourteen at the time when he asked me to help him with long division. He showed me two problems and was upset when I used other examples to explain the math to him. I explained carefully and had him do the division step by step. After I was done, he was able to do his homework, as well as all the other more difficult problems in the exercise. If I had only showed him how to solve the two problems he had for homework he would not have understood the mathematics, nor would he have been able to solve other long division problems. His words were: "This is so easy it's a joke". You must teach with the same purpose in mind and equip your staff with more than just the solution to the problem they face.

⚙ Tool 12: Selling skills

I joined a life insurance company as a salesman for a few years in my late twenties. Actually, we preferred to be called "Representatives". The reason for this career move was to make a lot of money in half a week while I built up an engineering business to design and supply tooling to the motor industry the rest of the week. It did not work that way and I had to work really hard at the selling job for more than just five days a week. I never even started the tooling business. After two years I realised that my dream could not be realised. I was not happy selling and returned to the engineering profession. A lot of people reasoned that I wasted those years. I treasure my selling experience.

You will need to sell your ideas to your staff and your management. If you are poor at persuasion and at closing deals, you will struggle to get what you want. Many a good idea died or was stolen by someone else with persuasion skills simply because the originator was not skilled at selling. In a later chapter, you will learn how to persuade people by understanding them and what is important to them. Persuading others is not a trick or slickness of tongue but a genuine behavioural science to study and apply.

➤ <u>Tool 13: Computers and Software tools</u>

A computer is a machine. A computer cannot do anything by itself, but computes do what you instruct them to do through programs. The computer on your desk will have specific software to record and processes data, write reports, emails and do computations. You must get to know these programs as quickly as possible. There are some programs that are basic to any business. These are: Spread sheets; word processors; operating systems; email and financial software. Make an effort to know them as soon as possible.

Computers are the most efficient time wasters known to me. I have seen people, including myself, sit and "work" on computers while their main jobs, or "A" activities (see a previous chapter on A, B and C activities), suffered. Do not fall into this trap if you have a computer on your desk.

To make sure you do not fall into the trap of "playing" on your computer all day, get one of the activity trap sheets mentioned in a previous chapter and complete it for a few days, including the time you spend in front of your computer. At the end of each day you must evaluate the activities carefully to see if you were wasting time.

There are some safeguards against wasting time that you can implement in your department and for yourself:

- ☞ If you find you are entering data or doing other mediocre things, you must delegate those activities to a secretary or administrative clerk, for example.
- ☞ Skill yourself in Macros or ask somebody to help you automate repetitive tasks, graphs and other processing if you have to do it.
- ☞ Make sure you are not duplicating any work or data. Most companies are networked and all computers are linked so that other people's work can be seen by you and vice versa.
- ☞ Use the internet during lunch times to search for private things and to read emails.

☞ Try to avoid giving your work email address to your friends.

☞ Tell your friends you have no interest in jokes and other stuff forwarded by them via email.

☞ Remove all games from the computers of those who work for you. I found highly paid people playing Solitaire for hours.

☞ Do random checks on the history files of the browser. If the history file is clean you must assume that something is not right and the user is hiding something.

☞ If a person changes the screen when you approach them you can assume they were busy with something against the rules.

And a final test to make sure you are not wasting time. Agree with your superior to remove the computer from your desk for a week. Ask the secretary to check your mailbox and print any work-related mail. Then scribble an answer and return the paper to her so she can answer the mail. All other data entering must be done by somebody else. After the week you will know how much computing must be done only by yourself. Beware – the answer will shock you. You will have much more time to do your "A" activities. Now do the same for those you manage.

Case study: Old computers:

In 1997, the company I worked for upgraded their computers just before I joined them. They did not throw away the old computers because they still worked and others could use them because they are so-called "free". One of these landed on the desk of the electrical supervisor, who had no computer at the time and did not need one. Very soon he was so busy on the computer that he requested me for an upgrade. His work suffered from his absence in the factory.

It took me five minutes to realise that the work he was performing on the computer was nothing of importance and to remove it from his desk. After that, he was spending his time on the factory floor where he could solve and prevent problems. From that experience we made a new policy: whenever there was an upgrade I gave the old computer to the person who used it before, complete with operating system CDs and manuals, to take home or give away. I charged a very small fee to formalise it. This way all old computers left the company and no additional needs were born resulting in time wasters.

What do we learn from this story?:

- People are very creative and will build a job around something they enjoy doing. If this is not in the company's interest you must stop it and prevent it.

- Computers are time wasters. If your job is done on the computer you must be careful not to get side-tracked by internet and games or social networks.

- If your actual work is not done on the computer and you have a computer on your desk for email (and other things like reports), you must be very careful not to get involved with non-core activities. You can easily be busy on a computer for hours not doing constructive work.

- Old computers are old. Throw them away or give them away with the operating system and if there is software is on it make sure the you give the licensed discs with it, otherwise remove the software.

Tool 14: Authority

You must understand that if someone is promoted from within the ranks it will be extremely difficult for that person to manage his previous peers and friends. They will expect favours and they will not respect the authority of their new manager simply because he was one of them. The new manager will not know how to handle this situation in or outside of work. There are three ways in which I have seen large companies deal with this issue:

1. The first and the best way are to train the new manager in all the skills necessary to manage the staff and process. When he is

ready, he is promoted into a different factory or department. On arrival he is introduced to the staff as a manager or supervisor and the relationship kicks off on the right level.

2. The second is when there is no other factory or department to send the new manager to or it is not possible for whatever reason. In this case the staff will be forced to address all managers in a formal manner. They are not allowed to use first names with any superior. There is usually a specific dress code or "uniform" for each rank, for example a dust coat for a supervisor, long sleeves and tie for a department manager and so on. This culture is mostly terrible to work in and reminds one of the military. The effect is that a distance is instantly created between the manager and the staff. At the same time the manager must now call his new peers by their forenames. This can be difficult because they were recently his seniors. This establishes the new manager on the new level very quickly. The results are good. I have worked in such an environment for five years.

3. The third way is to keep the relationship informal between the promoted manager and the staff. There will be a few months of awkwardness and then some distance will grow between the manager and staff. This manager will need a lot of assistance and visible support to get established as a manager in the new position. This method is the least productive and carries a high risk.

If you were promoted from within the ranks and must now manage or supervise your former buddies or friends I suggest you create some distance between you and them. Start by not eating lunch with them; do not socialise with them after hours. It will be for your own good. If you do not do this you will end up protecting them if they fail you and you will lose your position or even your job. There will always be something to give up for promotion. Manage this carefully.

Your position will give you the authority you need. You must embrace that and use it positively. Do not change into a policeman (unless you are in the Police force). Nobody respects a person merely because of rank. Respect is earned and goes hand in hand with the authority you have and the way you exercise it.

⚙ Tool 15: Registers

This is a simple tool that does not take a long time to complete if you do it regularly. You simply cannot remember all information for a week. Use the registers to log data, events, and non-events and so on. Instruct your staff to do this for every area under your supervision. This will also help you to delegate your non-KPA work. See the chapter on KPAs and A, B or C activities.

⚙ Tool 16: Communication

A colleague of mine once said that the company we worked for operated like a mushroom farm. He explained:

> "Management keeps us in the dark and feeds us manure".

I thought the colleague hit the nail right on the head. Make sure this is not said about your communication. You have some responsibilities regarding communication:

☞ Find out what formal communications are expected of you from your manager.

☞ Find out what formal communications must be given through to your staff.

☞ Use notice boards. Write the date the notice is posted and the date it must be removed. If your notice boards look the same every week nobody will see anything on it.

☞ Have regular feedback meetings. Keep it short and stick to the rules as discussed in one of the "tools" regarding meetings.

☞ Never give information through to your staff that they cannot handle. For example, in some cases the staff will hear what the turnover was and interpret it as profit. In one such a case we almost had a strike because management told the workers the company had no money for increases. Rather give the profit or achievement versus targets as percentages.

☞ Give information all the time. Do not wait for the meeting you have once a month. You can talk to your staff while they work. They need to be informed.

☞ Feedback on the performance versus the production targets is very important. If you link bonuses to performance you can use this to your advantage to keep the staff motivated to take up the challenge.

☞ In some cases you must have confidential discussions. Make sure there is a room, office or place for this where the worker will feel comfortable. If a discussion was confidential make sure it stays that way.

☞ Establish a communication channel from your workers to you and encourage open and frank communications. Make sure to reply and follow up on every point raised.

☞ When you communicate instructions to your staff, be factual and clear. Always ask the person to tell you what you have just instructed him to do. This way you will make sure he does not "interpret" your instruction. This applies also if the instruction is in writing.

☞ If you communicate with people from cultures other than your own, make a study of that culture to understand how they communicate, how they build their sentences and much more. It will help you, especially if they are not fluent in your language. In some cases you must stick to the simple present tense for example. Never use slang word "guys" if you refer to persons or "Jo'burg" if you refer to Johannesburg. Speak clearly and slowly if you realise that a foreigner does not understand you and try to limit your vocabulary to his as much as possible. The objective is not to speak English like the BBC news readers, but to get a message across so that the other person understands you.

☞ Different people or cultures may interpret the same thing differently. To illustrate this point, where I worked I called together all the role players of the departments we worked with. I gave each a blank sheet of paper and a pen. They had to think of something and draw only the outline. I took up the sheets and handed them out so that each person had another paper with an outline from somebody else. They had to fill in the detail without any consultation with anybody. After this I held up the sheets, one by one, asking who made the outline and what it was they had outlined. The laughter was heard in the next building because some outlines were interpreted very differently from what the outlines originally stood for. From then on they all spent an extra few moments making sure that what they wrote or asked for was interpreted correctly.

Tool 17: Secretarial or similar service

The secretary is not a tool, but a person who provides a great tool in the form of a service. In a previous chapter we discussed A, B and C activities. You must do your best to delegate your C activities, non-core activities, to the secretary, as your C activities can be the secretary's "A" activity and her main job.

Other services that can take administrative work away from you can be the Human resources, Finance, Logistics or Buying departments and so on. If they cannot do the work you need them to do and are willing, you must teach them.

Tool 18: Code of conduct and laws

Every country and company has laws and rules as well as a set of codes of conduct. You and your staff must respect these and live and work by those rules. Make sure your staff know the rules and keep them to it. If they do not abide by them, you must discipline them using the company procedures. Remember that the purpose of discipline is to change behaviour, not to get rid of people.

Be honest and fair to your staff, your managers and your clients.

Tool 19: Knowledge of peoples' behavioural patterns

You have to realise that all people are different, but their communication styles can be grouped into a few styles. If you apply your knowledge of how they function and communicate, you can change your own style to communicate better. This is so important that I want to say it again in another way. You are the one who must change your communication style as you work with each person. You must change your style to theirs. More about this in a later chapter, but for now you must realise that this is a useful tool.

Tool 20: Knowledge of yourself

Know your own ability. Never tackle a job bigger than you can handle without asking for help from your supervisor or manager. In order to grow you will have to take on tasks you have never done before and tasks that eat at your nerves.

Do not let anybody tell you that you are no good at something simply because that is his perception of you. There are many managers who are threatened by their juniors and use this trick to push promising people down for a vast array of reasons. Know your attributes and limits and stand firm. Develop yourself all the time.

Tool 21: Problem solving and investigation techniques

You must realise that almost all problems can be solved by someone or a group of people within your reach. Do not let a problem get the better of you and do not think that you must solve all the problems by yourself. Stay in control of the process, even if the problem is big and an expert is hired to fix it. You must learn techniques to deal with problems in an efficient way. You must also know that the obvious is not always the solution. We will deal with this tool in detail in a later chapter.

There is a tool called "TOP 5" that can be used for solving problems. This tool is also in this chapter.

Tool 22: Stop jobs

In a previous chapter we dealt with the list of jobs you must have ready for your staff to fall back on if their regular work cannot be done for whatever reason. You need to be firm with this tool. It will ensure that the staff wants to do the regular task first. They will apply initiative and plans to do so if the alternative jobs on the list are less pleasant like, for example, cleaning.

Tool 23: Honesty and integrity

My father used to tell me he would not sell his name for all the money in the world. In my working life I have seen many people who did just that, sold their names for a little bit of money or favour by lying, cheating or robbing the ideas and initiatives of their workers to glorify and promote themselves.

You need to make it clear to yourself that you will never take or offer bribes in whatever form, never be dishonest, never steal, never cheat and so on. This is essential if you want to be a good example to your staff. After all, would you like your staff to do any of the above?

There is only one way to work with the people under your supervision and care. You need to be honest and ethical to a high standard. Act with integrity. If you fail to do this they will soon find out and you will lose their respect, or worse, they will follow your lead.

Do not use God's name in any form or reference to enforce your point or to add weight to what you say. Respect other people, their religions and their political views, even if they are not the same as your own.

In my travels I have seen senior people swear and blaspheme on a grand scale in my presence. A few times I requested them to stop this behaviour and they said: "It is our way, we mean nothing". It is for sure not my way and if they had any respect for other people they would not do it. To test the "it is our way" principle, I asked them if they talk like that in front of their mothers and the answer was always a definite NO. Never use bad language in front of people who you think do not understand your language. Many times they do.

Do not tolerate any person on your staff doing any of the above. Use the company codes of conduct to rectify such behaviour and promote good moral values and ethical behaviour.

There is a world-wide movement that was started in South Africa by prominent business people to be "unashamedly ethical" in their businesses, places of work and dealings with others. You can visit their web site to learn more about this movement at www.unashamedlyethical. co.za. If you want to you can join them.

Tool 24: Your appearance

There is much to say about power dressing. Few people realise the importance of this until you see a person dressed out of the norm or out of place. If you are a lawyer in a big law firm you will need to wear a formal suit, but if you are a supervisor on a building site you may wear denims and boots with a golf shirt and maybe the popular "three-day beard" look. Whatever the norm is for your environment is probably the right dress code. You can find many books and articles on the topic if you need to know more.

Make sure you are neat and clean. Make sure you look different from your workers if you are in a factory environment. It will help you to keep authority if you look and act like their superior or manager.

At the time of going to press all three of my sons are in university. I find it strange that the students go to class with bare feet and in shorts. One would expect that the higher institutes of learning would prepare the students to look like engineers, medical doctors and accountants. This trend started after I studied in the early '80s. This trend carries through to the work place. I have seen Engineers representing their company in a foreign country, wearing denims and a shirt not tucked in. This is considered a neat way to dress when you visit your friends on a Saturday evening, but in the business world it just does not make an impression if the person you meet is wearing a dark suit with a tie and you want his business.

A few simple rules for dressing:
- ☞ Dress like your customer or the person with whom you do business.
- ☞ Look your own age. A parent that dresses like a teenager will be laughed at rather than "get in" with the teenagers.
- ☞ Overdressing (too formal) may get you a "wow", but under-dressing can get you an "ouch" together with the suspicion that you are showing disrespect.
- ☞ To quote a friend: "Look around you . - maybe it's time to tuck in your shirt".
- ☞ Since I am not a woman, I am in no position to give them advice, but I do know this much: do not dress like you are going to the beach. If you want to be taken seriously in the workplace, dress as formally as you can and do not display your femininity too much.

➤ Tool 25: Self control

You must be in control of your emotions all the time. As a manager you will face many difficult situations. If you lose your "cool" in front of your staff, you may lose their respect, whether you lose the argument or not.

Stay calm and collected. If you realise you are losing control you must call for "time out". Make some excuse and set a new date to continue the argument or deal with the situation. This new date can be an hour away as long as it gives you enough time to compose yourself and gain perspective. Here is something I heard somewhere:

> "The person who loses his temper, loses the argument".

➤ Tool 26: Delegating skills

If you look at the kids playing in a schoolyard you will soon see which one of them delegates tasks to the others. Not all of us have such natural abilities. It can be extremely difficult to delegate a task to someone and see that person struggle with it or, worse, see that person do a second rate job of it. You have to be strong and keep the objective in focus. Help the person to understand and help the person to do it right without doing it yourself. Over time, the task will get easier for that person. You can always step in at the right moment and give support and help, but never take the task from the person's hands. This way they will do their own work and you will be free to do your own work.

I found that the main reason for not delegating work is that "I will do it better if I do it myself". This may be true, but you cannot do all the work yourself just because you can do a perfect job while eager, willing and qualified people stand around idle. Evaluate the overall objective and follow the following rule:

> Do not let perfection stand in the way of
> something very good.

Tool 27: Daily review

At the end of the day, evaluate the day and reflect on what was good
and what was not good. Some tasks may not have been done at all.
Some of what you did needs follow-up or you must do it again. You
need to think about the past day and use the result to plan the next.
If the next day is already planned, you will have to re-think and adjust
your plan. If you see that no amount of planning will get the job done,
you must get help, extra people or do whatever it takes to achieve the
goals. Remember to communicate the new plan to your staff before
they start their work.

Warning:

There will always be people around you that do not plan their days and
weeks ahead and then ask you to do all kinds of favours to help them
out of their problems. If you do this you will be in trouble. Maybe you
must help them, but do so in a formal way. Ask them to make a written
request, copied to your supervisor or manager and together you must
then re-plan all the work. If this is a "once-off" it is no problem, but if
this kind of interruption is regular you must ask your manager to deal
with it and train the other person to plan his work.

> Work not done + a very good excuse
> = work not done.

Tool 28: Time

In a previous chapter we dealt with the effective use of your time by
discussing the activity trap. The time management of your staff is an

important tool in your hands and the effect of wasted or used time will be multiplied by the number of staff you have.

Typical time wasters are:

☞ Absenteeism

☞ Smoke breaks

☞ Computers (refer to this tool earlier in the chapter)

☞ Coming late or leaving early

☞ Slowing down towards the end of the shift

☞ Starting slowly at the beginning of the shift

☞ Meetings that are not related to the core business

☞ Working slowly because of a lack of resources

☞ Waiting for resources and raw materials

☞ Private phone calls - make sure you have a policy regarding mobile phones at the place of work

☞ Procrastination

☞ Administration and gathering of information you do not need

The way to combat time wasters is to be very strict about time-keeping and other activities that are time wasters. Make sure work is done at full pace until the end of the shift or day. Make sure there are routines for collecting information at specific times. If your staff works shifts you must get them to do "handshake handovers". This means that one relieves the other from duty at the place of work without stopping the work or the machine.

What do you think of the following theory regarding smoke breaks?

Wherever I worked all my life there were smokers who took ten-minute smoke breaks every hour, hour-and-a-half or a few times a day. This can use up to an hour a day. In this time the non-smokers worked. I asked my manager for time off because I do not smoke. I suggested that I go home on a Friday after lunch time to take my accumulated "smoke breaks". The last time I suggested this to my manager, who was a smoker himself, he promptly told me that he was thinking of work while he smoked.

"OK," I said, "I will think of work while I cut my lawn every Friday afternoon or while I ride through the mountains on my motor bike." He was not impressed.

Just for interest's sake, in Johannesburg there is a company with a non-smoking policy has the following rules: If you want to smoke, you need to clock out, leave the premises and stand in the street to smoke on your own time.

Tool 29: Resources

Make a list of all the resources at your disposal and manage them well. If you do not know how to manage the resources you must ask your manager or the person in charge of the resource. These resources will include the important Six Ms that make a business work, as well as others more directly at your disposal:

- <u>Money</u>: Find out what the budget is, how it is calculated and how to control your part of it. The best person to help you will be the person in charge of Finance.
- <u>Manpower</u>: This is your staff and can be other people working in other departments. Remember to make a list of people who are experts in the field of your work on whom you can call for advice.
- <u>Machines</u> and tools that produce the goods your company manufactures.
- <u>Materials:</u> This can be raw materials as well as consumables.
- <u>Management:</u> Your managers who have knowledge and experience as well as other departments that give a service to your section.

☞ <u>Methods:</u> This can be recipes, procedures and standards.

⚒ <u>Tool 30: Criticism or Critique</u>

The purpose of criticism is to give feedback to actions and initiatives and to improve the result. Critique the actions or behaviour, not the person, and always lift out what was good, together with what needs improvement. Criticism must be honest but subtle and truthful or it can destroy the enthusiasm and spirit of the person you criticise.

Criticism on its own could be interpreted as that you are trying to look good at the expense of the person you criticised. To illustrate this you must recall the latest elections where one political candidate criticised the opponent. The objective is to persuade you that the other candidate cannot represent you and therefore you are left with only one choice. You must not do the same with your staff. Every criticism must be accompanied with help and advice. Make very sure you are on the side of the person you critique and the word "together" features very prominently in the help you offer along with the criticism.

> You can only do something wrong if you do something.

⚒ <u>Tool 31: Email</u>

Email is a fairly new communication method and there are no rule books for it. Let us therefore apply some common sense. I have found that the following works well:

☞ Always use capital letters for names and at the beginning of a sentence. Do not confuse "chat room" rules with email; they are not the same.

☞ Always answer within a day, even if you just say: "I received your request and will attend to it in a day or two". People know you will receive the mail they have sent you very fast. Some people ask for a "read confirmation". This is a reply message sent automatically stating that you have received and opened the mail. They will then expect an answer soon. The world of business is fast and immediate response is becoming the norm rather than the exception.

☞ Do NOT pass on jokes and other cute stuff. This irritates busy people and will get you into trouble. Many spyware and virus products are hidden inside jokes that are sent to all your friends. This is one of the methods with which spammers get your address to shower you with junk mail.

☞ If the sender or the topic is not something you expect, right click the mail and look into the headers or properties to see what it is about. Do this even if you know the sender. This will not open the mail and therefore not activate any virus or spyware hidden inside the mail. If you are still not convinced that the mail is legitimate, leave the mail unopened and write a new mail to the sender to ask what the mail is about. The golden rule is that you do not have to open a mail just because it is in your inbox. A mail with an attachment is highly suspicious and must only be opened if you are very sure that you need to read it.

☞ Do not set your mailbox to "Preview" the mail. This feature opens the mail to preview it. I cannot understand why the default settings of the most popular email software is set to preview mail, because it actually opens the mail and if a virus is present it will be executed. You have to deselect this feature in every mailbox you have if you want to reduce the risk of virus infection.

☞ Always make your subject something a computer cannot generate. There must be a personal item in there to indicate to your recipient that it is not a virus but a mail from a person that knows him or her.

☞ Do not think that because you know the sender the mail is safe. Viruses use other people's address books to fake senders. Be suspicious about all mail.

☞ Make sure you have an up-to-date anti-virus program and also be aware that those programs are counter active; in other words, they react to a virus after it hits. What does this mean to you? If the virus hits you before the antivirus program has a fix or can recognise it you will not be protected. Also, if the virus is one day old and you have not updated your antivirus program in the last few hours, you are vulnerable.

☞ Resize photos before emailing them. Do not send huge photos files unless graphic art must be done on them. Some email software has an option to resize photos. I recommend you use a photo-resize program like Photo Resizer Pro from www.ShowYourPhotos.com to resize photos in batches. This will save you a lot of time.

☞ Create folders in your Mailbox to store important emails separately from others. Email is considered a legal document and you must store it somewhere if you think you will need it for reference later on.

☞ You must realise that an email can be analysed to determine from which IP address (internet protocol) and from what computer it was sent, which route it followed, which computer received it and much more. In some cases, a printout is not enough because not all the above information is printed with the email.

☞ Never give your username or password to anybody. Mail from your computer is considered to have come from you personally. Other people can make a lot of trouble for you if they send out mail in your name. Change your password regularly. Search the internet on the topic of good passwords before you decide on your next password.

☞ Make sure your system date and time is correct. This will date your mail with the correct date.

☞ You can email yourself. I use this to remind myself of things I must do.

☞ Do a spell check on your text. In my case, I have to do it because the communication language in our company is not my mother tongue and I cannot spell to save my life. People find it very annoying if the male eye sent them is full of miss Takes. Also look for grammar mistakes. For example, there is not one spelling mistake in my previous sentence, yet it is full of mistakes and will confuse the reader.

☞ Ask the administrator to back up your data and email every day. If you are not connected to a network that can back up your data you must do it yourself. For this you need an external hard drive to copy the important folders with your data. Make sure you locate and back up the email folder. Ask for help if you cannot find it. Store the backup in another building.

☞ If you copy other people, use BCC to hide the list of recipients. I frequently get emails about product specials, which have been sent to all a company's clients and where all the recipients are listed in the CC section. This is valuable information given on a platter. Did you ever wonder where the junk mail sender gets your address? Just think of the mail your friends send you with all the names in the CC section. There is software that extracts email addresses from the mail you pass on to your friends and a lot of people make a lot of money selling your address to others who do email marketing. As a matter of etiquette, you can put the recipients in the BCC section and list their names inside your text. This way, the other recipients know who else received the mail without compromising their email addresses. Search "email BCC" on the internet to learn more about the solution to this problem.

⚙ Tool 32: TOP 5 tool

Are you producing 100% of the time with a 100% efficiency using 100% of the raw materials making 100% of the products at 100% quality? Perhaps not! If not, why not?

Call a meeting and ask your staff why they do not achieve the above. Maybe perfection is not possible all the time, but they have to strive towards it. See the expression on perfection in the highlight block at the end of this tool description.

Here is how to tackle your problems:

List the problems:

- ☞ List all the problems that they face. Do not let them say what they think. Let them write it on post-it notes. Give everybody the same colour and size. Give each person the same pen. They must write one idea or reason per note. This way they will not feel stupid if they list an unpopular problem or be victimised if they name a problem that someone else is trying to hide. The process must be anonymous.
- ☞ Collect the post-it notes from everybody by collecting them in a box or "hat".
- ☞ Remove the notes randomly and stick them on the white board.
- ☞ Put similar problems together.
- ☞ Ask the people to summarise each group of problems into one problem statement.
- ☞ Rank the problem statements from one to whatever, number one being the problem that is the biggest obstacle for reaching the 100% goals.
- ☞ The first five problems will be your "TOP 5".

Dealing with the problems:

☞ You and your staff must now tackle the first problem and solve it. It may be difficult and you may need to ask for help from others, but you have to solve it. Once you have done all you can to solve it you may start on another problem.

☞ Have a "TOP 5" meeting every week, say on a Friday afternoon.

☞ Look at the nature of the problems and invite people to the meeting that can help you. For example, the Maintenance Engineer, the Human Resources Manager or the Buyer to name a few. In the first "TOP 5" meetings I was involved in, we had one person from Brussels and another from Norway at the meeting via telephone conference. I was in Botswana.

☞ Ask yourselves if the first problem is still the number one problem and report on what was done. Help each other with advice and whatever else you can give. Think up new schemes.

☞ Keep minutes of the meeting. Make a copy of the minutes to your senior so that he knows that you are tackling the problems. I'm sure he will help you where he can.

☞ as soon as you tick off one problem you must move the others up and bring in the problem that was number 6 onto the list. Do this until the problems are trivial and you no longer need a "TOP 5".

Monitor everything carefully. As soon as you find that the questions regarding 100% efficiency or any of the others cannot be answered to your satisfaction you must reinstate the "TOP 5" tool.

> "It is the trivial things that make perfection, but perfection is no trivial thing."
>
> This quote is possibly by CJ Langenhoven (Freely translated by the author)

Tool 33: Statistics

Statistics is the study of the collection, organisation, and interpretation of data (definition from Wikipedia). This applies to production data and much more.

Try your best to gather data and get statistics for the processes and production you manage. This will indicate outcomes for actions or events based on the average history.

You can use it in conjunction with the database tool mentioned above. If you think that something will help you if you have data on it, simply record it for a while and test your theory.

If you have it, the following are possible uses of statistical data:

☞ Average employment period for the workers in your section. This will determine your training plan and effort to avoid staff vacancies.

☞ Time spent by yourself on the factory floor related to production outcome, quality problems and the scrap rate. Use this to see if there is a relationship and find the critical point, then plan your day around it.

☞ Accidents in relation to the time of week or day. Use this to see tendencies and combat them.

☞ Production rates in relation to time of the year. See what effect public holidays and summer season have on your production and combat it as far as possible.

☞ Performance of the team in relation to the hour of the day. You will find trends linked to lunch times, shift changes and much more.

Every action has an effect. Repeated actions have repeated effects. Record the actions and effects and make sure you find and understand patterns. From these patterns you can make fairly accurate predictions.

Guide the actions in the direction from which you will get the best results.

Case study: Never shortcut the statistics.

Let me point this out by quoting an example from the time I sold insurance in 1988: I had the statistics recorded and used it to understand that *for* a commission of ZAR300 I had to make ten phone calls to prospects, from ten calls I got three appointments and from that I got one sale with an average commission of ZAR300. Interesting, so what process did I manage most? The phone calls. I had to make those calls. The statistics were accurate because I took the data over a long period. In fact, I could decide how much I wanted to earn and calculate back how many phone calls to make. I also realised that if I got four sales from my ten calls, there would be a time when I would have to make thirty calls without any sales if I follow the same type of leads. It would have been no use if I got happy about the sales and went to the beach for the rest of the week. In order to help me manage this process I had to get seven rejections a day before my work was done. The rest followed like the white waters follow a speed boat. You too can use statistics and manage the inputs in such a way that you will influence the outcome.

Tool 34: Cause-Remedy book or database

Every time you solve a problem you gain experience. The problem is that the person with the experience is not always present the next time the same problem occurs. Make a folder with alphabetical divisions and an index to cross reference every entry. Every time a problem is solved, enter it into the cause and remedy book and make as many cross references as you can so that other descriptions of the same problem will all lead to the same solutions page. Better still, if you can create a database for this as well, the whole factory or office can look it up and add to it. The book is still important because factory workers normally do not have access to the computer networks during the night. The next time you or anybody else has a problem, first consult the cause and remedy book and see how it was solved previously. Edit the solution with new information and solutions. This will save you a lot of time.

This is also discussed in the problem-solving chapter.

Tool 35: Written instructions

When you instruct somebody they will hear what you say and try to remember it. They will rely on their short term memory. In another tool I suggested that you use a small notebook to write down items you need to remember. The fact is the short term memory lasts for a minute if you are lucky. When you give instructions, take your pocket book and write what you want, then tear out the page and give it to the person. This way you solve a few problems:

☞ Neither he nor you have to rely on short term memory.

☞ The worker will not interpret the instruction before trying to remember it. It is important to know that when memorising things your brain "hooks" the thing you want to remember to similar items in your existing memory and when the memory is recalled some confusion is possible.

☞ You can also email the instructions to the worker if he has a work email address to finalise the instruction and make sure all misunderstandings are out of the way.

☞ You save the whole "repeat after me" situation that may embarrass the worker.

Checks to make sure you have the benefit of this chapter:

	Yes	No
I have "put away' my old tools:	☐	☐
I will teach my staff to use their tools:	☐	☐
I have built up a new toolbox with the tools listed in this chapter:	☐	☐

The _________________ tool is the one most important for my job and situation right now.

The _________________ tool is the tool I will find most difficult to use.

I will use the library, internet and other resources and study the subject of management: ☐ ☐

I will ask my colleagues for criticism and use it to improve: ☐ ☐

I will apply my knowledge rather than talking about it: ☐ ☐

I am using a diary or I will start doing so today: ☐ ☐

I will buy or get a small pocket book and pen to carry on me from today: ☐ ☐

I will use my email effectively: ☐ ☐

I will be honest and behave in an ethical manner towards my staff and my clients: ☐ ☐

I will make a list of people I can call for help:

Name:	Phone number:	Help with:

Team building part 1 – All aboard

Think of your favourite team sport. There are a lot of people making that team. There is a captain, a coach, a manager and so on. I follow every football world cup series and I am amazed by the news afterwards about how the coaches were fired because the team did not perform well. Take note, the coach, not the captain, not the manager, and not any of the players. Why the coach? I do not know, but we can look into the matter and maybe we will find out.

Team Goal:
A team is, by my definition, a group of people that competes and needs to win against an opposing team for a reason linked to glory, fame, money, honour or some award. In your job the people you manage is the team. You are the captain, the coach or the manager, depending on how many levels you are removed from the actual team of workers that are tasked to achieve the goals. You need to understand what the goals are. In order to do this properly you need to understand the business map of the organisation you work for. From this map you must determine the goal or the part of the business you control, or ask your superior if there is no clear map. We discussed the business map in a previous chapter.

You must know the goal of your team, what they must achieve, how much of it they must achieve, when to deliver it, where to deliver it, to whom to deliver it, what documents to give with it and what documents to collect when it is delivered.

Team Strategy:

If you know all the above, you can break each goal into smaller goals or steps. Break each of those steps into even smaller steps or into the parts that make it up. You need to break it down until you reach the point where you know you are in control, or how to control it.

To put together a team strategy, you need to plan activities for each of your team members to make sure the parts that make up the goals are addressed in the correct order, at the right time, in the right place, with the correct raw materials or resources and that the relevant documentation is completed on paper or put into a computer.

Make sure you assign the right person to the right job.

Who are the team players?:

The next chapter will deal with different communication styles. This knowledge of your staff and their preferences will help you know how to employ them efficiently. Study this chapter and apply the knowledge. You will not regret doing so. You will see people giving their best with a smile and a skip in their step.

Team support:

Any successful team has a host of people supporting them. In sports, this group is made up of managers, owners of the clubs, specialist trainers, medical staff, psychologists and so on.

Who supports your team?

- In an industrial setting you must be supported by the administration staff. Few people know this, but the administration staff is there to bring goods and resources together with the staff and machines so that a product can be produced.
- All other departments.
- All your senior managers are there to support you.

In my past experience I had many problems because the administration staff thought production was there to serve them, while it was the exact opposite. The matter of A, B and C priorities, as described in a previous chapter, must be understood by all. The business activities must be mapped and the "main road" clearly marked. For example: If the raw materials you need to complete a job are not on site because the supplier needs to be paid before he releases the goods, the accounts manager has no bigger priority than to sort this problem out, even if he is busy preparing statements and month-end results for the management meeting in two hours. Few understand this.

Think carefully about who can support you and your team and make a list. This can be the Human Relations Officer, the Accountant, your superior, the Logistics Manager, the Maintenance Manager, the Secretary, the Forklift Driver, the Store Keeper and so on. From your business map you can look at each incoming item, including information, and use the person in charge of that item as a support person. Get the commitment of each supporter and make sure they understand that you may need their help in order to achieve your goals.

Ask each of them how they think they can help you to achieve your goals, the inputs, the procedures, the methods, the money, the staff and whatever they or you can think of. You MUST ask them because they are the ones who know exactly what they have to offer you.

Case study: The noise in the shaft of a pipe making machine:

I visited a pipe producing factory in Spain in the year 2000. They were making good pipes, but a noise came from the main shaft that sounded like *the* moaning of a bear. We, the technical staff, knew that it was the inner shaft that touched the inside of the main shaft and that it needed to be lifted by about 5mm. We planned to do this when the machine stopped. There was no danger or threat of possible breakdown because of it.

While this noise was going on the company accountant walked past the machine on his way to the raw material stores. He heard the noise and slowed down, listened carefully, determined it came from inside the machine and walked straight to the machine supervisor to inform him that something was wrong. The supervisor had some difficulty convincing him that this was not a bad noise and that it would be fixed as soon as they stopped again.

What do we learn from this story?:

- What is significant about this is the fact that the accountant did not just walk past. He was interested enough in the A activity of the company to know that if the machine broke down the production would stop.

- A person removed from an actual job can still keep the core activity in mind and help to point out if he sees an obstacle.

- You can help others if you can.

- Do not wait to be asked for help, just offer it.

- If others offer help, be thankful, even if you do not need it. You may need their help in future.

Keep your distance:

There is a saying that goes something like this: "You cannot see the wood for the trees". You need to be able to stand away from the team effort while it happens so that you can see what is going on and manage it. If you have a job inside the team, where others need your outputs as their inputs, then you may not be able to see the wood for the trees. This is a recipe for disaster. Make sure you are free from the activities in order to manage them. If you are the team coach, you cannot be the captain.

Game plan:

In order to have a game plan you need to assign each person to a responsibility or task that will work together to reach the goal.

In order to effectively do this you need to study the next chapter first and continue with team building in chapter 8 once you understand 100% what chapter 7 is about.

To be continued in chapter 8 ....

Adapt yourself to communicate effectively

I recently bought a new fax-printer-copier-scanner. I had to study the manual in order to set the date, print my fax number on top of outgoing faxes and so on. It took me several minutes to navigate through the menus to find the features and then to find a way to set my preferences. I had to find out how it worked. It did not bother to find out how I wanted it to work. People are the same. Each person works in a certain way. Some of those ways are embedded into their beings. Sure, a person can adapt to your way of working, but it may not be fast, or pleasant, or easy, or even possible if the person is the proverbial round peg in a square hole. In other words, if you know the natural attributes of a person you can manage him in a way that will be very successful for both him and you. This chapter will deal with this matter and help you to achieve just that. Read on....

We are all different. Some of us like a lot of detail while others only want the bottom line. Some are "all or nothing" while others are happy in the middle. I hope you are not trying to place yourself in one of the above because it does not matter.

This chapter will change your life for the good if you silently APPLY the knowledge from this chapter or it will make you a very unpleasant person if you use the knowledge to marginalise people, or if you use the knowledge as a stick. I will explain........

Let's say a new staff member joins the company where you work and you are introduced to this person.

During the first moments after the introduction you will observe a few things about the new colleague. For example:

- ☞ The gender of the person;
- ☞ The age of the person (younger, approximately your age or older than you);
- ☞ The position or rank of this person relative to your own;
- ☞ The race or ethnic group;
- ☞ The fashion of his clothes; to name a few.

Your method of communication will alter slightly because of what you observed. This is a good thing, unless you are disrespectful. It does not mean you are false. It simply means that you respect the other person. If you are a man and the new colleague is a woman or older person you will most likely adjust your manner positively to show more respect. This is applying the knowledge you have gained about that person by your observations. In this example a bad way to use the knowledge that you have of the new person's age would be to say to the colleague: "John, since you are the junior and younger than all of us, you will have to take stock this weekend." A good way to use the knowledge would be to consider that John is young, most likely needs extra overtime pay and has a lot of energy. Then you ask: "John, would you like to earn some extra money by taking stock this weekend ?"

You will always observe others and you will always form an opinion of them. This chapter will help you do it constructively so that you will be able to use the information to improve the interaction and communication between you and the other person. Some may argue that you must be a professional to analyse others. True, but you will not be analysing anybody, you will just be observing them. In the example above, the company doctor examined the new employee and in his file would be the exact age, weight, height, gender, race, allergies and much more. I can see that he is tall, but the doctor knows his exact height.

> You do not need to be a professionally qualified scientist to observe and estimate the few attributes you need to in order to adjust your own behaviour to meet that of the other person.

One more important point before you read the rest: NEVER tell the other person that you have observed anything about them. This is marginalising them. Never say: "Because you are a woman you can take my seat". Just say: "You are welcome to take my seat". She knows she is a woman, trust me!

The example and explanations above are about physical attributes to explain the point that you will and can observe things about other people. This chapter is more about behavioural attributes. I hope you understood the point I've made above because it applies in the same way. USE the observation to adjust the way you relate and communicate without letting the other person know that you know something about them. The objective is to communicate better. It is as simple as that.

<u>WARNING:</u>
The purpose of this chapter is NOT to observe yourself and then demand a change in others to accommodate your preferences. This happens a lot and the people who do this are generally the people we do not like. Always keep this in mind. You are the one to observe the other person and adjust yourself in order to communicate more effectively with your peers, your seniors, your staff, your family and anybody else you deal with. For this reason this book will not assign any time to determine your style or preferences. This is not about you; it is all about the other person. To illustrate this point more, imagine you plan to visit

a Spanish-speaking country. You will have to learn how to say "good day" or "Hello" in Spanish if you want to communicate something in their language. You will learn to say "Buenos dias".

> "Good morning" in Spanish will be "Buenos dias" if you are English, "Buenos dias" if you are Swahili, "Buenos dias" if you are Portuguese, Italian, Russian or whatever. It does not matter what language you speak, it matters what language the Spaniard speaks.

The same applies for the styles. You need to observe in what style the other person communicates and then communicate in that person's style, regardless of what style you are. So therefore it does not matter who learns how to say "good morning" in Spanish, the outcome is the same: "Buenos dias".

Style and behaviour

In the same way you would observe if somebody is tall or short, male or female you would observe whether they are assertive (bold, brazen, forceful) or not, show emotions or hide them. You will not analyse them, just observe and make mental notes. I said in the "foreword" of this book that you do not have to understand the technical workings of a car's engine in order to drive it. The same principle applies here. You do not need to be an industrial psychologist to observe behaviour and apply your observations.

What is of extreme importance is to understand and accept that other people are different to you and they are right the way they are. Their style and behaviour may not be like yours. You can alter your own style to match theirs with one objective only, and that is to allow the other person to be comfortable with the way you ask, tell, request, instruct or relate to him. Just imagine your manager is a bottom line type person and you know this. If you want him to decide something, you will give him the bottom line while you keep the detail in reserve for when or if he asks for it. Does it matter if you are a "bottom line" person yourself? NO!! This may be very difficult for you to do if you believe he needs the detail. Trust me if I say you will bore the socks off him if you present him with endless detail and he will most likely lose interest before you ask the question. Knowledge in this case is the power to communicate effectively. This does not mean you are false or that you trick people. It means you apply this knowledge to improve the communication and get the desired result with the best efficiency.

Some facts about people's style and behaviour:

☞ All people are different and all differences are acceptable and correct. Just because they are different from you does not mean they are wrong.

☞ There are many ways to describe the behaviour of people. We will use the way they communicate as well as behave to assign one of four styles to them. This will be their main observed style and the one you adapt yourself to in order to communicate effectively with that person.

☞ All people behave in all the styles to a greater or lesser degree. You will observe the most obvious style they use in your environment.

☞ People adapt their styles according to circumstances. This can be for their work, or a crisis or simply the relaxed environment of their homes.

☞ The four different styles where people mostly apply themselves will each have a basic set of attributes you can recognise.

☞ Once you know a person well enough you will fine-tune your observations and improve your effort to adjust your communication style to match theirs.

☞ You can dedicate a life's study to this subject and not know it all. This chapter will be enough to improve your effectiveness and change you from a person who probably applied your own style to all people, to someone who appreciates and recognises differences in those you live and work with.

☞ THERE IS NO SHORTCUT. YOU WILL HAVE TO WORK THROUGH IT ALL SLOWLY AND CAREFULLY IF WANT TO UNDERSTAND IT.

Please note the following:

You will observe people in a particular environment, for example, at work. This does not mean that they will behave and communicate the same way in another environment like at home or at a party. I, for example, communicate and behave differently at home and at work simply because I had to adapt and discipline myself to what is necessary in order to perform my work, which is technical and detailed. In my case it is easily done because I have only a few more points on the "show" emotions side than on the "hide" emotions side of the diagram below. I have a high assertiveness (boldness, brazenness, forcefulness). I will give an example: The Monday after a wedding, a colleague who also attended the wedding said to me: 'Hey Piet, I never knew you to have as much fun as I saw you having at the wedding'. If you ask anybody at work if I'm a fun person they will say no; if you ask my family they will say yes. In my job at the time as a maintenance and engineering manager there was no time for fun and games. This is called "adapting to circumstances". It is a skill some master well. If you do not adapt your style to the needs of your job, you may struggle with your work. It is a known fact that very few people are in jobs that exactly match their personality styles. Some people are doing this without realising it. Some people experience a lot of work stress because of this difference.

Application:

Knowledge is useless unless you apply it. In this case the knowledge you are about to gain will be dangerous if you do not apply it correctly. I will stress this point several times as you read on. I have seen many situations where this knowledge was converted to a stick used for hitting people. The application of what you are about to learn will follow later in the chapter. Please make a huge effort to understand it, and then apply it carefully.

Naming the four styles:

I will try not to label the styles. The danger of that is that you will box and marginalize the people you observe and lose focus of the objective. If you really want to label other people, use labels "A" and "F". Use "A" to label everybody else because all people are "A-OK" the way they are and use "F" to label yourself because you Failed to realise that people cannot be labelled simply because you observed a few things about them.

I will use the two most easily observed attributes to describe the four styles and name the styles based on what you observe.

Diagram:

We will use a diagram to plot the styles described later on in this chapter. It is important that you draw such a diagram for each person you want to observe to make notes of your observations.

Emotions: Hide or show:

It is easy to see if a person shows or hides emotions and feelings, especially if you have known the person for a while. The proverbial "poker face" for example can be happy or sad and nobody will know it. Some people like myself walk around with a complete report of their well being written all over their faces.

Assertiveness: Ask or say:

It is also easy to observe whether the person asks many questions or gives a lot of orders or instructions. For example, spot the difference in the following two examples where a parent tells a child to pick up his clothes.

"Pick up your clothes"

"Will you pick up your clothes?"

In neither case does the child have an option to refuse. The first was said with high assertiveness and the second with low assertiveness. These attributes are described in much more detail as you read on.

See the diagram below:

<u>NOTE</u>: I have been asked by many people to put the main attributes of each style on the diagram. I cannot do this because it will be an injustice to the people described in the style. I suggest you take a sheet of paper for each person you want to plot and draw the diagram, then write down the attributes you recognise in the relevant style. This way you will not have three words describing 60% of the population.

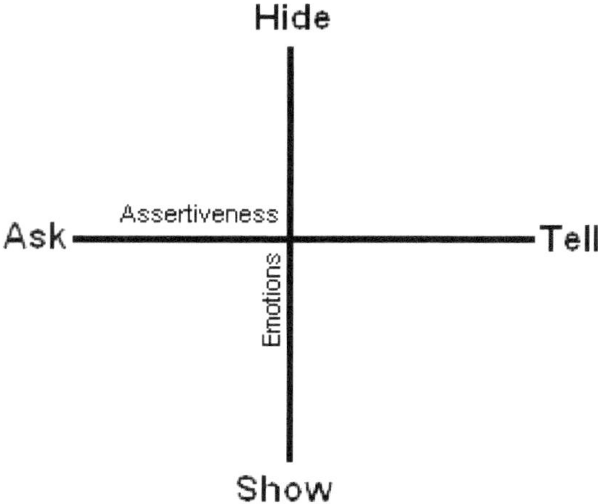

You will now, for example, describe a person's style you OBSERVED as: "Tell and Show" or "Tell and Hide" or "Ask and Show" or "Ask and Hide". Always refer to the "assertiveness" axis first in order not to confuse yourself or others who will read this book and then discuss it with you. Also, all references must be made using these descriptions of the styles when you describe the behaviour you observed.

Remember: These are OBSERVATIONS, not analyses. Leave analysing for the psychologists.

Determining behaviour or style:

Let's get started by noting down general attributes for each group. You can copy the pages that list these in the relevant quadrants and keep a copy on each person with whom you wish to improve your communication or relationship. Update your observations as you learn and observe more. First impressions always stay for the ignorant, but a clever person will learn and adjust all the time.

Tell - Hide (High assertiveness and hide emotions):

- When they speak they use their finger to number facts, events, instructions etc and sentences usually start with "In the first place, …"
- They keep a high degree of eye contact,
- They lean forward when they speak.
- They point their index finger at the people they address.
- They jump to the conclusion as soon as possible.
- They prefer the "bottom line".
- They are task orientated.
- They interrupt others and themselves.
- They are very neat and orderly.
- Their desks are clear and organised.
- They delegate tasks easily and effectively
- They like to take charge.
- They are strong willed.
- They can make quick decisions.
- They are quickly bored.

- ✔ They are very time conscious.
- ✔ They prefer "open" instructions without "brackets".
- ✔ They tend to ignore rules.
- ✔ They have lots of initiative.
- ✔ They challenge the status quo.
- ✔ They are drawn towards conflict.
- ✔ They do not compromise easily.
- ✔ They are confident.
- ✔ They like changes.
- ✔ They like challenges.
- ✔ They are "NOW" orientated.
- ✔ They prefer "MY way".
- ✔ They want to know "WHAT"?

<u>Tell - Show (high assertiveness and show emotions):</u>
- ✔ They are enthusiastic about what they do.
- ✔ They see the big picture.
- ✔ They have many dreams and schemes.
- ✔ They keep a high degree of eye contact,
- ✔ They appear relaxed.
- ✔ They prefer the "bottom line"
- ✔ They interrupt others.
- ✔ They are very disorderly.
- ✔ They delegate tasks easily and effectively.
- ✔ They like to take charge.
- ✔ They can take quick decisions.
- ✔ They are quickly bored.
- ✔ They ignore the status quo.

- ✔ They are creative.
- ✔ They have initiative.
- ✔ They are confident.
- ✔ They like changes.
- ✔ They like challenges.
- ✔ They are influential.
- ✔ They are oblivious to rules.
- ✔ They are "people" orientated.
- ✔ They are FUTURE orientated.
- ✔ They prefer "The FUN way".
- ✔ They want to know "WHO"?

<u>Ask - Show (low assertiveness and show emotions):</u>

- ✔ They are very loyal.
- ✔ They are good at relationships and befriend everybody.
- ✔ They have great endurance.
- ✔ They can perform repetitive tasks.
- ✔ They prefer "brackets" (a clear description and limits of the task).
- ✔ They are great team players.
- ✔ They follow rules.
- ✔ They prefer the status quo.
- ✔ They avoid conflict at all cost.
- ✔ They are critical.
- ✔ They will compromise their own ideas or plans to benefit the group.
- ✔ They submit to leadership.
- ✔ They are polite.

- ✔ They show respect.
- ✔ They are "people" orientated.
- ✔ They finish tasks.
- ✔ They live in the PRESENT.
- ✔ They prefer "The EASY way".
- ✔ They want to know "WHY"?

<u>Ask - Hide (low assertiveness and hide emotions)</u>:

- ✔ They have great endurance.
- ✔ They can perform repetitive tasks.
- ✔ They need a clear description of the task.
- ✔ They are critical.
- ✔ They make decisions based on facts, not emotions.
- ✔ They prefer the status quo.
- ✔ They have intimate knowledge of the rules and follow them.
- ✔ They consider all detail in what they do.
- ✔ They pay attention to detail.
- ✔ They make slow and good decisions using all possible information.
- ✔ They are polite.
- ✔ They have a long attention span.
- ✔ They live in the PAST.
- ✔ They prefer "The CORRECT way".
- ✔ They want to know "HOW"?

A quick method to plot a person you meet for the first time:

Any person can be observed fairly quickly. Note, I say observed, not analysed. If you do not know a person and want to adapt your communication to their main style you can use the lists below. This is only a quick preliminary observation based on things to look for when you meet a person and will be enough to adjust your style of communication. If you deal with the person a lot, use the lists above for a more accurate placing.

<u>High assertiveness:</u>

- ❑ They make a lot of eye contact.
- ❑ They number the points using their fingers as they speak.
- ❑ They will indicate a chair for you to sit on.
- ❑ They interrupt others and themselves.
- ❑ They take charge without being asked.
- ❑ They shake hands.

<u>Low assertiveness:</u>

- ❑ They are polite.
- ❑ Their eye contact will never make you uncomfortable.
- ❑ You may sit anywhere if you enter their offices.
- ❑ They offer drinks and whatever they can to make you comfortable.

<u>Hide emotions:</u>

- ❑ They look businesslike, neutral or even unhappy.
- ❑ They get to the point without a lot of casual conversation.
- ❑ They are focused on the task at hand.

<u>Show emotions:</u>

- ☐ They make casual conversation.
- ☐ They remember your name.
- ☐ They show photos of their children or pets.
- ☐ They share personal detail.
- ☐ They are interested in you.

You are now the most dangerous person on the planet, armed to the teeth to marginalise and exploit others, but you will not do that - Right? You will read on and learn how to apply this knowledge and bring out the best in other people.

Case study: Sales:

In my late twenties I sold insurance. Insurance is a difficult thing to sell simply because the buyer does not see the product and may never have the **benefit** of it. Because I am an engineer, I thought all people would be interested in the detail and workings of the policy, especially how the interest on savings is compounded. I was wrong.

To be more effective I attended a seminar on the subject of communication styles to help me understand my client quicker and communicate in his style. There was a drastic change in the number of sales versus appointments after I started applying this knowledge. In an appointment to sell insurance, or in fact to sell anything, there is only a minute or so of introductions and pleasantries in which the salesman can observe the buyer and adjust his style accordingly. I only had to make a very general assessment in order to determine how I would present the sales talk. For example: with or without the detail, how much eye contact to make, and how much pressure will close the deal. A few minutes was all I needed to make a huge difference in my style of communication.

What do we learn from this story?:

- People are different and you either believe it or you do not. If your income depends on a theory you'd better investigate it.

- You now have proof that this is not just a theory, but something that was used by the author with huge success.

Case study: Communication:

In a recent job, my manager complained that one of his colleagues frustrated him to the point that he avoided him. The colleague apparently talked too much about non-work stuff, sat typing on his computer for a long time after my manager entered his office and seemed to be reluctant to respond or help immediately. I offered to help. I observed a "tell-hide" style with my manager and an "ask-show" style with his colleague. These are exact opposites. Because my manager had no knowledge of this subject he expected everybody to communicate, act and react like he did. My advice to him was the following:

"Next time you enter his room, say hello, sit down and do not talk. Let him complete the thing he was doing. This will prove to him that you show respect for what he is presently doing.

"While you sit there, note the family photographs on his desk and the other memorabilia in the office.

"He will stop whatever he is doing as soon as he realises you are respecting him and his time.

"You must first do some relationship building. Ask about how he is and ask about the photos and pictures on his desk. This will only take a few minutes.

"Then discuss the work and you will be surprised at the co-operation you will get."

A few days later my manager reported that he had applied the advice and it was amazing how it had turned out as I predicted.

What do we learn from this story?:

- Your style is not the only style

- Never think others must adapt to your style, even if you are there superior.

- Study the subject and apply one thing at a time to see the result.

- Expect improved relationships as others experience the respect you show them by adapting yourself to their style.

Case study: Antique shop with low sales:

Both husband and wife worked in this shop. They were the owners. The husband was the one with the passion for old furniture and he was really knowledgeable **on** the subject. Their problem was that sales were very low regardless of the stock and traffic through the shop. I asked him what he did when a customer walked in the door. His said he would wait while the customer browsed to get a good idea of everything in the shop.

He would then walk up the customer to present himself and offer help if they wanted it. Then he would retreat a short distance away and wait.

Most customers walked out soon after this.

I lectured them both on the four types of style and how to recognise them as well as how to respond to each. We also dealt with sales closing techniques. There were practice sessions. It took three hours.

For interest sake, I taught them the following about the way people buy things. Note, it is a general rule only:

<u>Tell-Hide:</u>
They decide they want something, look for a fairly good deal and buy it directly.

<u>Tell-Show:</u>
They will see something that they did not know they wanted and buy it impulsively.

<u>Ask-Show:</u>
They befriend the salesman and then buy what he recommends. They trust their friends.

<u>Ask-Hide:</u>
They decide that they want something and then do extensive research on the article. They will test the salesman on the detailed knowledge they have before they buy. If he fails, they will buy somewhere else.

A month later my friend reported that sales were up where he wanted them to be. He recalled an example of a man who had walked in and had walked straight to a small table. When the man stopped at the table my friend was right there and asked him if he liked the table. "Yes, how much is it?" He quoted the price and closed the deal by asking if he should deliver or if he would take it himself. This sale was very hard for my friend because he thought the person should first have asked for all the history and detail about the antique before he decided to buy it. Not sharing this information was difficult and he actually felt he had cheated the person. Had he given all the detail the person would most likely have walked out before he was halfway through it. The owner's style was mostly Ask-Hide.

What do we learn from this story?:

- Others are different from yourself.

- Other people are right the way they are and do not have to change to your way of thinking.

- If you want success with others, study them and find out what makes them tick, then supply it or sell it to them.

Application of this knowledge about the styles:

The above heading is in bold and very big simply because it is so important. There are many people in a team, each of who has a specific job to do so that the goal of the team can be reached. Regardless weather you are the coach or the captain for the process or people you manage, you must understand that the differences in people must be celebrated and used for the benefit of the team.

So why celebrate the differences? Simple: the members of the team will be able to fulfil the different tasks better if they are different. In the case of the four different groups of people we discussed, each group has strengths and weaknesses. A "strength" is something the person is able to do as part of his nature and you will not have to help a lot in that area. Refer to the case study below, about my son Pieter. A "weakness" is something the person does not do naturally and with which he needs prompting or help. It is not a negative attribute; in fact, a weakness for one could be a strength for another, so make sure that you understand this concept before using or applying this knowledge.

<u>Case study: My son Pieter, the story teller at four years old.</u>

One of the sales managers where I once worked attended a seminar on sales techniques and related skills. The presenter showed them that it is possible to talk about anything with confidence. He asked the people to select any ten of about 300 slides from a box and to put them in any random order in the projector. Without prior knowledge of the slides, he then started to do a presentation related to the images in the slides. He made up his story on the spot, talking from one slide to the next regardless of whether they were related or not. He then taught this skill to the delegates. To some it is natural and to others not, as in the case with this manager. If he wanted to be able to do this he would have to move right out of his comfort zone and it will be very difficult. In fact, I would not recommend that you apply somebody so far out of their comfort zone unless there is some emergency.

The manager in this case behaved in the "Ask-Show" area. For him relationship is very important and he would rather die than talk a lot of nonsense to somebody he respects. On the other hand, the lecturer was more a "Tell-Show" type and could do this unconsciously because he was having fun.

To prove my point at the time, I asked my then four-year-old son, whom I knew behaved in the "Tell-Show" area, to tell me about a squirrel. I was not completely finished with my request when he started the most imaginative story about a squirrel and how he went looking for food for the babies and so on.

What do we learn from this story?

- In your team, you can identify the natural communication preferences and the skills people can apply without extra effort.

- Try to match the people with the tasks. This will not be a 100% match all the time and some people will have to do tasks or jobs not exactly within the natural preferences.

- If a person has a task that is difficult for him, you must assist him to do it, much the same way the spell checker on my word processor helps me to spell better. For example, not being able to spell did not stop me from writing this book.

Spreading of different styles:
If you take a sample of one million people you will find that the division is not in four equal parts. The bigger the sample the more accurate the assumptions.

Let's see how many of each style we need on our team:

Tell-Hide:
These are task-orientated people who are happy to be in charge and thrive on pressure, take responsibility, can handle conflict and like to take up a challenge. They make up roughly 1/8th (about 12%) of the population.

Tell–Show:
These people live in the future, dream up new non-existing things and can get others to help paint their sand castles. They make up something between 1/8th and ¼ (about 12 – 25%) of the population.

Ask-Hide:
These are critical people, capable of dotting the "i's". They challenge others and keep the world in check. They make up roughly 1/10th (about 10%) of the population.

Ask-Show:
These are relationship driven people and they are the "worker bees" of society. They are steady, do not like changes, are loyal and do work that keeps the economy going. We need lots of them. They make up a little less than 2/3rd (about 60%) of the population.

You will note that percentages do not add up to 100, but then the above will be a little different for every sample you take.

<u>**Case study: Two detail-oriented people on my staff:**</u>

In a factory where I was the Engineering and Maintenance Manager we started from nothing and brought a bunch of old machines from Norway, the Middle East, Botswana *and* South Africa together in a forty-year-old building in Johannesburg. It was a nightmare because we started producing as soon as some of the old machines were plugged in. These machines broke down so much that we effectively rebuilt them on our maintenance program within the first year without a budget for the work or parts. The Safety Program was another problem because our new MD forced us into buying an extremely elaborate safety program with huge administrative demands. I am not somebody who likes detail work, nor anything repetitive, nor a lot of administration. So what did we do?

In order to plan and execute the maintenance we bought software to plan the work, flag schedules, store and transform the data into something we could use to improve all the time. The setup of the database, as well as the setup of the schedules, needed a special person. I found one who did this as if he was born to it and in the process of looking for him I made sure he was an Ask-Show style person. Why did I do that? Go back a few pages and look at the list of attributes of this group. This man did this work very well. One of his other tasks was to be the mechanical supervisor. For this, his profile was not ideal but, because I knew it, I supported him in the areas where he fell short so that the work was done as planned and to the expected level.

As for safety, I hired an artisan who behaved in the Ask-Hide group. He had a natural ability to get into detail and be meticulous. He kept registers and did all the inspections that were required at the specified intervals. The secretary did all the administration related to the safety program. I had no chance to do any of those tasks even with special effort. I had better things to do and delegated this work.

What do we learn from this story?

- You cannot be all things to all men.

- You will manage many things that you cannot do. Hire the right people for those jobs and manage them.

- In a football game, the goalkeeper cannot be the striker.

<u>Case study: The business consultant and his quiz:</u>

In a company where I worked all the managers were called to a training session where we were handed a quiz. The quiz had several complicated number sequences with gaps that had to be completed and there were some problems to be solved, etc. All of it had to be done in a specific time, so there was also some pressure. It was a good challenge for me and for some of the others. The stopwatch started and we got stuck in. After about five seconds one of the managers threw down his pen and sat there with a grin, twenty seconds later another, one minute later yet another and so on. The consultant noted down the names in the order that the managers put down their pens. By this time, the rest of us got wind that there is something fishy and looked over the rest of the questions. The last "question" was a statement that said "You do not have to answer any of the above to get full marks for this quiz". I realized I was being analysed by this little quiz and kept answering the questions until I was the last one doing it, just to make sure the assumption he made was an assumption.

AssUMe = Makes an Ass out of U and Me

He explained to us how important it was to read the whole task before we started it. The test did tell us that important fact, and it also told us a lot more than that, which the consultant failed to pick up on. Nor did he point out that in a team there is a need for the person who jumps to the end, but there is a bigger need for those who get stuck in and do the work until the finish. I fear to think what our senior management did with the information about who was first, second or last.

Let me explain more:

We are all different and our makeup causes us to behave differently. Because of this behaviour it is possible for others to spot and recognise our preferences. This test made it easy. "John", the guy who saw the last question almost immediately showed that he is a critical person and needed to make an overview before he committed himself. I started at the top and worked my way down because I am a task-oriented person. Some made it to question 12 and they proved to be very thorough.

They continued to work their way down the list regardless of the fact that it was obvious that the others knew something they did not. The people who like to have clear instructions to start and finish a task believed in the spirit of the test. The people who are time-conscious or critical looked the whole thing over to plan it so that they would finish within the allocated minutes and saw the last question. In a team, you need all of these people.

The test should never have told anybody he was right or wrong, but that we were all different and that this very fact was our strength as a management team. This was a good opportunity to explain the roles and the needs for each different member on the team. In this case "John" was the Logistics planner and he was in fact good at it, others were Quality Control, Production and I was the Engineering Manager. We all had very different roles and functions in the same team.

What can you get from this story?

- When you train your staff they must be uplifted, not downsized in the process. Never rub in the fact that they do not have the knowledge they are about to get. They know it. That is why they are there.

- Never put the focus on how clever you are. This will put them in a bad spot and they could close up and miss your training. In fact you are not (I am not) all that clever; you just know this one thing better than they do, that is, if you do know it better.

- Never use a simple questionnaire or a single test to categorise people. The result may or may not be worthless. The next time any of those people, including me and now also you, fills in a questionnaire they will all look at the last question first. Does this mean the "Ask-Hide" person has been transformed to a "Tell-Hide"? Surely not, but it may be assumed by the person marking the test. Experience helps us to be better at what we do. It does not change our psychological behaviour.

- Know your people and their styles and make sure you adapt your instructions so that each person gets it 100% right every time. If an "Ask-Tell" person, for example, needs information that is in the summary of a document before he reads the body of the instruction, you must put the summary on the top of the first page.

What can you do with this information?

APPLY IT, but how?

Let us take the attributes of each style and deduct from it what you can do to communicate better. Please note that you must ignore your own preferences.

<u>Tell - Hide (High assertiveness and hide emotions)</u>:
They keep a high degree of eye contact.
> Look at the person so that he knows you are listening and that you understand.

They lean forward when they speak.
> Do not step back; it will be a sign of weakness.

They point their index finger at the people they address.
> Do not be intimidated by this.

They jump to the conclusion as soon as possible.
> Be firm. if you agree with their summary it is good. If you disagree with their summary, agree to their "conclusion" with a "but what if you consider this ..." and explain the point they missed. In other words, do not confront, but redirect.

They prefer the "bottom line".
> Start your documents and discussions with a very short summary of where this is going and what result you intend. You may be surprised that it will mostly be enough information for this person.

They are task orientated.
> Get to the point, keep to the present task.

They interrupt others and themselves.

>	You may also interrupt them if you make a short powerful statement.

They are very neat and orderly.

>	You must match this if you want their respect. If you are not neat or orderly, discipline yourself a little bit or pay somebody to clean up for you.

Their desks are clear and organised.

>	Give them things in their hands. Do not just drop it on their table or desk. Find their "inbox" or a dedicated area for putting things.

They delegate tasks easily and effectively.

>	Be careful that the tasks you give to these people are not immediately delegated further without responsibility.

They like to take charge.

>	Let him take charge if you can afford to do so and watch him from the side until you are sure he is doing it right.

They are strong-willed.

>	Do not fight this, guide it.

They can make quick decisions.

>	This makes them good managers in this area, but you have to give a lot of feedback so they can learn from the results. Keep a close eye on the decisions they make.

They get bored quickly.

>	Keep them busy or they will busy themselves.

They are very time conscious.

>	Do not waste their time. Make sure there is enough work lined up for them.

They prefer "open" instructions without "brackets".

> Tell them what result you want rather than how they must do it.

They tend to ignore rules.

> Help them by telling them to study and obey the rules. Put the rule book in their hands. Do not ignore them if they step out of line and disobey rules. They must obey rules like everybody else.

They have lots of initiative.

> Tap them for ideas and evaluate the options. Give credit where it is due.

They challenge the status quo.

> Allow them to "test" the present situation and if possible look from outside the box.

They are drawn towards conflict.

> Use them to resolve conflict.

They do not compromise.

> They may die for what they believe and may see compromising as a weakness. Explain well and convince them with facts if you want to change their ideas and beliefs.

They are confident.

> Always question what they do or say because it will sound like the truth even if it is not.

They like changes.

> Do not be afraid to suggest change. Let them manage the changes.

They like challenges.

> Challenge them to get them to do something.

They prefer "My way".

>If you disagree, use words like: "but what if you consider this ...". In other word do not confront, but redirect it so he thinks it is his idea.

They want to know "WHAT"?

>Tell them what. Please note that you need to speak the truth, not just because this group needs it but because it is the right thing to do.

<u>Tell - Show (high assertiveness and show emotions)</u>:
They are enthusiastic about what they do.

>Use them to influence others.

They are future orientated.

>Involve them in planning.

They see the big picture.

>Do not put them in a box by limiting their ideas and plans.

They have many dreams and schemes.

>Listen

They keep a high degree of eye contact.

>Do the same, they need to know you are with them.

They appear relaxed.

>They do not get "stage fright", use them for roles where they can work or speak with people.

They prefer the "bottom line".

>Start with a summary.

They interrupt others.

>Interrupt them and redirect them to the point.

They are very disorderly.
> They thrive in chaos. Do not judge them if you are the opposite.

They delegate tasks easily and effectively.
> Give them more work or take tasks from them and make sure they do it right if they delegate the tasks you give them.

They like to take charge.
> Be careful because they do not necessarily complete tasks.

They can make quick decisions.
> They may consider only the issue or person in front of them and may tend to forget everything else. They need help to remember other important issues.

They are quickly bored.
> Keep them busy, but allow them a bit of freedom.

They ignore the status quo.
> Help them if it is important to keep things the way they are.

They are creative.
> Use them to help with non-regular problems and projects.

They have initiative.
> Do not discourage them if they share their plans and dreams.

They are confident.
> Use them for selling ideas and influencing others.

They like changes.
> Change things regularly.

They like challenges.
> If you want them to do something, challenge them.

They are influential.
> Use them to influence others.

They are oblivious to rules.

> Help them. Do not let them get away with ignoring rules just because they are not important to them.

They are "people" orientated.

> They need to interact a lot with others.

They prefer "The fun way".

> Make it fun and they will be on board.

They want to know "WHO"?

> Tell them the names of people and other players to get them involved.

<u>Ask - Show (low assertiveness and show emotions):</u>
They are very loyal.

> Do not abuse this loyalty. Honour and reward it.

They are good at relationships and befriend everybody.

> Spend some time on relationship activities to get their trust. Make sure they do not socialise too much.

They have great endurance.

> They will stay to the end.

They can perform repetitive tasks.

> They are not easily bored with the job.

They need "brackets". A clear description and limits of the task.

> Give enough information, what you want and do not want, how much, when, etc. Do not let them guess.

They are great team players.

> They will compromise their own ideas and preferences for the greater good of the team.

They follow rules.
> You can sleep peacefully.

They prefer the status quo.
> You can save on redecorating. Do not make unnecessary changes.

They avoid conflict at all cost.
> They need some protection if bullied by others.

They are critical.
> They question changes or new things. This is good for you and may stabilise your decisions if you are a quick decision maker.

They compromise their own ideas to benefit the group.
> Make sure the "loud" people do not speak all the time in your meetings and help this group to air their views and ideas.

They submit to leadership.
> You can rely on their loyalty and that they will follow orders and instructions.

They are polite.
> Great attribute. This does not mean they agree.

They show respect.
> Great attribute. This does not mean they agree.

They are "people" orientated.
> Help them focus on the task.

They finish tasks.
> Do not give new tasks too quickly. They prefer one job at a time.

They prefer "the easy way".

> They may cut corners on the difficult parts of the work. They may submit easily in order to keep the peace. Sometimes this is not good if a persuasive person gets his way.

They want to know "WHY"?

> Tell them why. Be honest. If not you may break their trust and their hearts.

<u>Ask - Hide (low assertiveness and hide emotions):</u>
They have great endurance.

> They need to do a perfect job.

They can perform repetitive tasks.

> They will stay in the same job and will strive to improve all the time.

They need a clear description of the task.

> They need a lot of detail in order to be comfortable that they are doing the right thing and they are thorough.

They are critical.

> They question changes or new things. This is good if you are a quick decision maker.

They prefer the status quo.

> Do not make unnecessary changes.

They have intimate knowledge of the rules and follow them.

> Use them to learn specifications and other detailed rules your products need to comply to.

They consider all detail in what they do.

> They need to be managed to finish their tasks because they get pinned down by detail. They also tend to do everything themselves. Help them to delegate tasks.

They pay attention to detail.

> Use them to check things like documents and work for completion.

They make slow and good decisions using all possible facts.

> The often try to avoid taking a decision if they are not 100% confident about it and may even prefer that others take the decision for them. Do not do it, give them facts and detail or the means to get the right information. Get involved in the decision making process otherwise nothing may happen. You must explain that perfection should not get in the way of something very good.

They are polite.

> Great attribute

They have long attention span.

> Great attribute. They focus on the job, even if its gets boring.

They prefer "The correct way".

> This is good but you need to manage it because it can also mean they never do anything unless it is perfect. Perfection can get in the way of a very good job.

They want to know "HOW"?

> Tell them how.

What we just did here could be considered reckless or even dangerous because you may now be equipped with knowledge that you may not apply in the correct way. I have given enough warnings and special requests so that you hopefully understand the dangers of this knowledge in the wrong hands. I encourage you to read this chapter again and again and think about each style, making very sure the majority of attributes fit the person to which you want to change your communication style. Then study the application for that person. You may also ask the person some questions in order to fine-tune your assessment.

If this subject interest you a lot you can study it in more detail. Search for "Industrial psychology". In the back of the book I have some references to my resources if you want to get more from there.

<u>Understanding the behaviour of a cow:</u>
Many years ago my friend visited his parents where they lived on a farm. His father asked him to help him the next day by loading a cow onto the pick-up truck. He suggested that they start at nine o'clock because he wanted to leave with the cow at eleven. It normally took his father two hours to load a cow.

The next morning my friend took fifteen minutes to load the cow. His father was very impressed and asked him how he did it. "Simple, I pulled the cow away from the truck and gave just enough slack so the cow "pulled" herself backwards onto the truck".

Checks to make sure you have the benefit of this chapter:

Yes   No

I will study and consult with my staff until I am sure what their communication preferences are: ☐ ☐

I will see if my team members are in jobs not suited for them and do all I can to divide the workload to achieve the best work fit: ☐ ☐

I will manage meetings in a way to get the ideas and plans from the Ask-Hide and Ask-Show group of people, not just from the assertive people: ☐ ☐

I will not take my own style as a benchmark for "good people" or "correct behaviour": ☐ ☐

I will disregard my own preferences in communication and adapt to the style of others in order to communicate better: ☐ ☐

8

Team building part 2 – Lift off

We continue from the first Team building in chapter 6.

Now you have gained a lot of knowledge about the behaviour and communication preferences of your team and you will be able to apply and use this knowledge to improve your team in many ways.

Your team's game plan:
In order to have a game plan you need to assign each person a responsibility or task, each of which will work together to reach the goal.

In order to effectively do this you need to study the previous chapter. Apply the age-old "round pegs in round holes, square pegs in square holes" theory. This may not be possible because of particular skills that people already have. In this case apply the skills to the right task, but keep in mind where you need to provide extra inputs to make everybody do the best they can. In months and years to come, cross-train the staff so that they can be switched round and each person can finally be in the job that fits him best.

The game plan involves all the players or, in your case, all the workers. Call them together and show them the business map of what happens in your area, what inputs are there and what the desired outputs are. Each person must understand his role 100%.

The game plan is simple if there is no opposition. Like in any sport, if the opponent does not show up and your team plays against nobody they can do as they like without following any plan. BUT in reality there is always an opponent and you really need to have a good plan of action to beat them. In the workplace there is also an opponent to beat. This opponent has many names, for example: time, costs, raw material supply, unmotivated staff, sick leave, power failures, go-slows, strikes, poor quality, broken machines, slow internet, bad connections and many more.

The plan you and your team must make, must focus on how to handle each of the "oppositions" they may face. A plan beforehand is better than a plan made when the disaster happens.

Do not make the plans yourself. Use your staff or team to help you come up with the plans. Give them ideas, probe the ideas they bring to the table and steer the whole thing into a workable plan of action.

Note the following when you make plans:

- ☞ Do not let perfection stand in the way of something very good. You may set your sights high, but keep a realistic approach that is within the capabilities of your team. It may even be a stretch goal. Make good plans to get good results. How do you eat an elephant? One bite at a time.
- ☞ There is usually no single saviour or hero in a team. The whole team must put ideas and plans on the table.
- ☞ Make sure every member has the same understanding of the goal. Understanding the goal is not the same as having "heard" you say what the goal is. Multi-cultural teams need more explanations to be sure that what they hear is what you said or meant.
- ☞ Understand and apply the concept of synergy (where the total is greater than the sum of the individuals, for example 1+1=3)

☞ Learn from the ants. No individual ant can survive on its own. They are team workers. In fact, an ant is regarded as a cell in an entity, not a body on its own.

☞ As in any game, focus on the activity that scores the points. This means that some of your staff may need to be setting up while others need to complete the task. Everything must work towards the goal of your production.

☞ Make sure that the game plan has a strategy for each thing that can go wrong. This is an action plan.

Trigger the action plan:

The game plan must be followed by all people involved. Monitor the results and keep making small changes if you have to. Nothing can be predicted 100%, so the plans you make will rely on assumptions and forecasts that may or may not be 100% correct. If something goes drastically wrong, an action plan must be executed. You need to have something that will trigger the action plan.

The action plan can be triggered by some event, shortfall or whatever the "opposition's" name is. There must be an agreed signal or a message that should reach all the members of your team and each member must know what plan is being activated so they can do their part. An example of such a plan is the "fire drill". If a fire starts somewhere there is an alarm that everybody recognises. Everybody should know what to do and they will either leave the building, grab a stretcher or fire extinguisher or do whatever task they were assigned to do.

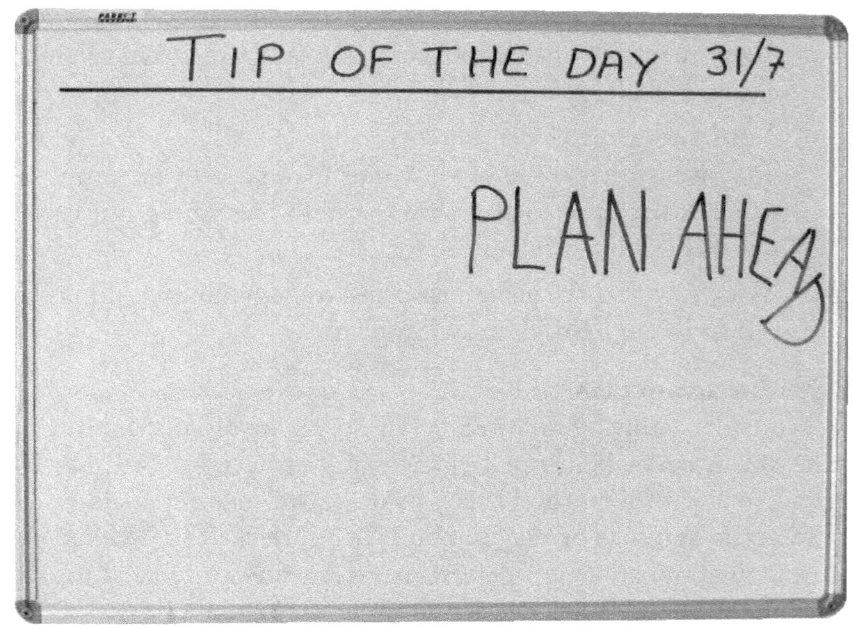

Is this notice board for real? Yes, and it makes a point.

Plan the work, then work the plan:
To make a plan is easy, but to execute a plan takes discipline, dedication, motivation and a huge effort.

Do not let any kind of outside influences change your plan. Other departments may not have a good plan and may ask you for changes in your plan because they need this or that urgently. In many cases you must oblige simply for the greater good of the company, but if this becomes the norm go and see your senior manager and tell him that this is upsetting your plan. Offer to help the other department with planning in the way you did your planning. Complaining alone will get you nowhere; go to your superiors with a solution.

Night shift:

If your team works in the night you must really be keen on making sure the production plan is executed. In the night you and your team, or just your team, will be alone. The supporting staff that we mentioned in chapter 6 will all be asleep. Certainly you can call them, but if you call them too often because you were not planning ahead properly you will get yourself into trouble.

<u>What can you do?</u> (Not all the remarks below may be applicable to you, so get the point and think of your own situation and make your own list)

☞ Make sure that all the raw material stock is drawn from stores before they close for the day.

☞ Ask the maintenance department to do checks on the machines, especially on the parts that have a history of breaking or failing in the night.

☞ Make sure all the equipment and raw materials that are needed to complete the work are on site.

☞ Go to the other departments that will interface with yours and make sure they are ready.

☞ Have a plan at hand just in case one of the night shift staff members calls in sick. Unfortunately, they mostly call after the shift has started and the previous shift has left. Create a culture of advance warning so that you can re-appoint some staff to make sure the work is done.

☞ Go to QC department and make sure they are ready to do all the checks so you will not have to wait for results.

☞ Go to the departments that will receive your goods and make sure that they are ready.

☞ If there will be a product change in the next shift, or even some days ahead, make sure all the equipment and tooling is serviced, ready and set up within the specifications.

In a pipe factory where I worked in 1994 one artisan showed up every afternoon at 4pm to check the machines, in particular the Venus resin guns. He would reset each needle to make sure it opened well and closed shut 100%. There were several maintenance people, but he was the only one doing this work in advance. We asked him why. His answer: "I am on standby this week and prefer to sleep at night rather than to be called out to fix gelled resin guns".

What do we learn from this story?:

- Forward thinking saves time and money.

- Unselfish behaviour benefits the team. In this case the artisan missed the overtime and call-out pay. This could be why others did not do it.

Checks to make sure you have the benefit of this chapter:

Yes   No

I will think of every possible hurdle or problem that will interfere with the work my team must do. To do this I will involve them and ask their inputs: ☐ ☐

I will let my team help me make a strategy, or game plan, to overcome each hurdle or possible problem: ☐ ☐

In the event that a hurdle that we cannot overcome comes up, my team will resort to the "stop jobs" mentioned in an earlier chapter: ☐ ☐

9

Training your staff

The best reward a teacher can ever get is when his student overtakes him. For example: nothing will give me more pleasure than to know that after you read this book you became a better manager than I ever was because this book will hopefully inspire you to read more, research the subject of management, enrol for a course and become far better than this book can make you. This is my dream for you.

Should you train your staff or hire them already trained and save a lot of money and time? For some jobs, like accounting, where the work is essentially the same in many organisations, you may be able to hire fully trained staff but for most other jobs you will have to find a person with as best a fit as possible and then train that person in the specifics of the job you need him to do. You can also head-hunt the perfect person from another company, but this is expensive and regarded as ethically wrong in some circles.

There are pros and cons for both, depending on the time and money you have, whether or not similar industries exist in your area and much more. Nevertheless, regardless of what you do or how you hire your staff, you will end up training them in some way or another.

When do you train your staff?

There is formal training in a controlled environment and there is "situation training", or "on-the-job-training". You need to do both.

<u>Formal training:</u>

This is where you explain the theory of something using notes and examples and explaining what you need them to know - much like this book. You need to be well prepared for this training and you need to give them notes or the opportunity to make notes while you teach them. Make the notes short and to the point. Keep your lectures interesting. Combine practical work or on-site visits to keep it relevant. It is a well known fact that very few people ever look at handouts after the lectures were given, so for this reason you should take a test at the end. Doing this will set the urgency level of the training, motivate them to make their own notes and will force them to study for the test. This is much more efficient than just giving a lecture.

<u>Situation training:</u>
Remember the management style I mentioned in a previous chapter called "management by walking around"? This is a typical activity for the rounds you make. When you see people struggling, teach them by telling them what and how, then showing them by doing a SMALL part of the work. They must then do the work as you have shown them while you watch and make sure it was understood. If they understood, good. If not, show them again and again and again and again and again...

DO NOT DO THE WORK FOR THEM. THEY WILL LEARN NOTHING. .

EXPERIENCE IS CAUGHT, NOT TAUGHT.

Make a training schedule:
Make a list of all the TASKS that are needed to do the work in your area of the business. Note that I once again refer to the "area" of the business. This is the work your team must do. Make sure you have a map of the business or a very clear description of the work.

Once you have the list of tasks, make a list of the SKILLS that are needed to complete the tasks to the required level.

Now put the names of the people or staff who have those skills next to each task.

Take a different coloured pen (or font, if you do this on a computer) and write the names of people you need to teach any of those skills to in order for them to do a better job.

Make a training schedule so that your staff will be well prepared and qualified for the work. Also start with cross-training. This is where you teach the skills of one person to another so that they can do any work. This is very useful in case of emergencies, or when one person is sick, resigns or is promoted.

Use your staff to train their colleagues

Your staff is much more willing and competent than you will ever realise. Use this willingness and ability to the benefit of all.

In your training program, ask a person who has mastered a particular skill to teach the others.

Cultivate a culture of teaching and training

There is a difference between a know-it-all and a teacher. The first we do not like, but the second we do. Why? Simply because a teacher, in his essence, strives to pass on all he knows and the best reward possible is when the student passes the master. You must cultivate an attitude where one person is proud to see another perform the skills he has. It does not get better than this.

Case study: Overhauling an engine at ages nine and eleven.

"Nonsense," is probably what you think now, but let me explain.

My father was a born teacher. Everything he did came with an explanation and an opportunity to try. He was a motor mechanic and like all mechanics he did private jobs. It was my job to hold the light during the evenings that he worked on cars. I was seven years old when I started helping my father by holding the light and passing the tools he called for. My brother was two years younger and he also helped my father.

By the time I was eleven and my brother nine, a man came to my father, asking him to overhaul his Austin Mini. This was in 1971. He only had the money to cover the parts. My father asked him if my brother and I could do the job if he wanted the work done for free. This way we could learn and gain experience while killing some time in our school holidays. Believe this or not, but my father never touched that engine. We took it out, stripped it, used plastic gauges to determine the wear on the white metal bearings and re-assembled the complete engine with new parts. We lapped the valves, bolted the cylinder head down to a torque of 145 foot-pounds, set the timing to fourteen degrees before top dead centre and the breaker points to seventeen thousands of an inch. When the car did not start after three swings he told us to look for the fault, suggesting we start at the distributor. We found the spark plug leads were 180 degrees out on the distributor cap. After this the engine started and purred like a cat. That was one of my biggest moments. My father did not seem surprised at all. See the photo below where we are stripping the engine. It is remarkable that we knew so much so young, but it was because we had a very, very good teacher.

What do we learn from this story?:

- A person is never to young to learn.

- Young people can be very responsible.

- Young people are also eager, so make sure this is not abused in terms of child labour.

- Children need to know something about the work of their parents. It gives security and helps with the career development of the child. In every factory I worked, I arranged "open days" for the families to visit the place of work of their parents.

- Sometimes you can do work for a friend or person in need without pay. In this case, there were other rewards.

- Boys or girls grow up to be adults. My parents did a great job preparing us for life, even if it was "work".

The author and his brother Jan, aged 11 and 9. Together they overhauled this Austen Mini engine in 1971. Was this an achievement? Sure, but not as much as the achievement by their father who trained them over several years while they helped him when he worked on cars. He never touched anything and the job was done 100%. No oil leaks and a happy customer.

Case study: Cooking by a ten-year-old.

I like to cook. I also teach everybody all the time, just like my father did. One evening in 2003 I had some lamb chops on the stove when my youngest son Pieter asked me what I was doing. I explained while he stood by with interest. I asked him if he wanted to do it the next time. When the opportunity came, I let him do it while hanging around, but not taking over. He added spices, etc. just as I had done it before. It came out well. Some weeks later I let him do it on his own. He started, but came to me saying the spices we used were finished. I told him to improvise and he asked, "what if it does not taste good?" My answer was: "Then we will eat slowly". He did a great job and it was very tasty.

 ManagementOne

What do we learn from this story?:

- When you teach people there must be a point where you trust them to do the job.

- Be ready to handle the exceptions.

- Keep in mind that there are some risks involved and be ready to jump in.

- Be prepared to carry the cost of the flop.

Teaching (This is Tool 11 in Chapter 5, repeated here)

The results of the department or section you manage are your number one objective. To achieve the results every person must do his work well. Unfortunately people get sick, get into accidents, pass away or move on. There is nothing we can do about that. When this happens somebody else must do that person's work with the same degree of efficiency, even if it is your own job. You must make sure that this is possible by teaching your staff.

A friend and mentor gave me the following advice as a young man: "If you want to make progress in your work and in life, duplicate yourself in others and work yourself out of a job". Apart from that my late father always taught me how to do everything he did. Later I realised he was doing exactly what my friend told me. Today I know the value of it more than ever before.

You must learn to do the following to be a successful teacher:

☞ Take stock of the skills and knowledge of your staff.

☞ Draw up a training program to give the skills and knowledge to those who need it by either teaching them yourself or hiring somebody else to teach them.

☞ Get written material like manuals, books, explanations on the topic and present it to the members of staff who need it.

☞ Use the company's training budget to buy training material and courses.

☞ Hand down your knowledge and skills to individuals.

☞ Ask others with specific skills to teach your staff.

☞ Make use of suppliers to teach you and your staff about their goods and technology.

☞ Attend trade shows relevant to your industry and brief your staff on what you have seen and learned to keep them enthusiastic and up to date. If possible take one of your best performing staff with you.

☞ Use those people in the team with more knowledge and experience to teach the others.

☞ Cross-train your staff. Make sure you move the people around so that every task is known to at least two people. Do not do this in a secret way, but make sure it is a formal process with training, tests, assistance, evaluation and recognition. This goes for your own job as well. You might like to think that only you can do your work, but if you do you are a fool. This is a harsh statement, but very true. The reality is that if you fall ill for a short period, or you must travel, someone will make sure the work is done to the expected result. Nobody will really take control of your position in a few days with such effectiveness that you will be redundant unless you are not doing your job well in which case you better study this and other books.

Teaching does not stop at telling somebody how to perform a specific task. It includes developing that person. You will soon see who on your team can be trusted with decision making and responsibility. Use them and mentor them without discouraging them. If they make decisions, comment truthfully. Never put them down by telling them six is better than their half a dozen just for the sake of correcting them. This will wear them down. I had a manager for more than eight years doing exactly that. Nothing I ever did found his approval the first time.

There was always something meaningless to change. This results in uncertainty and your staff will have to check with you before they make any decision. Be mature and trust your staff. Allow them to see the result of their decisions so that they can learn and grow in this area.

Records of training:
The people must sign a register to acknowledge the training they receive. Add the training notes to this when you file it. This applies to informal on-the-job or situation training as well. In some countries, like South Africa, there are Government funds that will refund a portion of the in-house training you do, if you have proof that it was done and if the workers benefits from it. It is also important to have proof in case a worker claims that he did not know something.

Finally:
Some people protect their jobs and their knowledge and they have good reasons, but I prefer the opposite. As I have quoted before, a friend of mine once told me that if you want to get ahead, "duplicate yourself in others and work yourself out of a job". This is what I've done all my working life. The fact is, if you teach others all you know, you are free to go on vacation, take a promotion and so on. Even if you leave your job for another it will be a good feeling to know that the work will continue without you.

If you are considering the cost of training, remember this:

If you want to hatch chickens you need to break eggs.

10

Safety and housekeeping

Safety must be an "always-on-your-mind" priority if you work in a factory, construction environment or where your staff works with any kind of plant and machinery or in dangerous environments, even offices.

People are the biggest asset of the company. They are in your care and under your supervision. It is your duty to ensure their safety.

Why do we use the word "house" keeping? Why not "factory" keeping? Simple: a house is a place that gets dirty every day and we clean it every day, or several times, or once a week, depending on what area it is. My kitchen gets cleaned twice a day, the bedrooms and the living area every third day and the garage once every six months. Why? Because we live there and if we do not clean the kitchen every day cockroaches and pests will make nests, germs will have parties and we will get diarrhoea or other diseases.

Your place of work should be the same. It must be cleaned in a cycle of time so that no dirt accumulates or builds up. In twenty years the floor must still be as it was when it was new, the cupboards clean, etc. Age is no problem, but dirt is.

Safety and housekeeping seem to go hand in hand. A dirty, untidy place is normally unsafe because the untidiness can be slippery, a tripping hazard, a fire hazard or represent an array of other dangers. An unsafe workplace will affect the output of the people and the machines.

There are several things you can do from today onwards to ensure a safe workplace:

☞ Make a list of all the safety aspects and assign responsibilities for each person. You are responsible for the safety, but they are the ones who must act safely, use the equipment in a safe way and so on.

☞ Make sure your staff sign for the safety aspects they are responsible for.

☞ Do a daily walk around with the staff members responsible for each area and inspect the area for cleanliness, stacking methods, obstacles and whatever you can see out of place.

☞ Look into cupboards randomly to see if there are any objects that do not belong there as well as to check the tidiness of the cupboard. Include electrical panels in your inspection (I found people keeping their lunch in electrical panels because they are warm).

☞ Note all stacking on top of cupboards and make sure it is removed.

☞ Do random checks on electrical equipment, ladders and scaffolding to make sure they each have a register and that they are checked for safety every month or as per the safety program guides.

☞ Make sure you have a trained first aid person on your team on every shift.

☞ Make sure the first aid box is stocked, sealed and available.

☞ Make sure the fire extinguishers are serviced and ready.

☞ Disallow all practical jokes and horseplay.

☞ Make sure you have a safety representative, one of your staff, on the safety committee. Help and assist this person to perform the duties by giving them the time to do inspections. Take note of recommendations and implement the necessary improvements as soon as possible. Rotate the representative at least once a year in order to expose all your staff to that level of safety awareness.

☞ Give regular safety talks on various topics. This does not have to take long. Quarter of an hour is enough. Let each person who attended the safety talk sign a register of attendance. This is for future reference.

☞ Encourage safety at the homes of your staff. An injury at home also impacts the work because, if that person is absent, you will have to make do with one less competent person.

I said earlier you must have the people sign a register to acknowledge the training they get. Add the training notes to this when you file it. If somebody gets injured you may have to provide proof that the person was trained and provide the contents of the training. If an accident happens, the accident investigator will ask for all the evidence. If the accident resulted in a death of one of your workers, the courts will use this information. Having proof is important, but even more so is the fact that you need to train every person for the job they do. This includes pointing out the dangers.

For the record, you can easily get statistics from you local government about the safety in your area. For South Africa, the statistics are horrifying. Almost one fatal work-related accident occurs per day. There are about 600 near-miss accidents to every fatal accident. Ask yourself: "Will somebody get injured, or maybe die, on my watch today?" and do all you can to make sure that statistic is not because of your management. You can do an internet search by searching the following phrase: "statistics of accidents in the workplace", then find your relevant statistics.

There may always be excuses if you present safety ideas to the management. If it will cost money, it may be possible that it cannot be afforded. Put your ideas in writing and attach an "approval for expenditure" with it. If it is rejected, the company MD or another senior manager must sign it and provide a reason, therefore taking the responsibility onto them if something happens. This is a "cover your behind" approach, but at least you did all you could to keep the situation as safe as possible.

Safety programs

In South Africa, where I live, we have several safety programs that you can buy. These will give you all the procedures and forms you need to make sure you do the right things and that you do things right. The sellers of these programs do audits and give ratings. In big companies, these ratings are displayed at the gate and it ends up being a priority of the MD.

These programs can be a huge burden on your administration. Be sure you know what to do and make very sure you delegate all the filling in of registers and other paperwork. A program like this can be a very useful tool if you do it right, or it can be an albatross round your neck if you do it wrong.

Make your own safety program:

You do not need an expensive safety program if you follow a few simple rules, read some articles and make a plan of your own. To do this you can consider the following:

- ☞ Get a copy of the health and safety act for your country and study it. You will find that it is not as complicated as you thought.

- ☞ Make a list of all the "safety items". This can be fire fighting equipment, tools and machines, electrical equipment, ladders, forklifts, hoisting equipment and cranes, housekeeping and pathways, stacking of raw materials and finished products, registers, incident reporting and so on.

- ☞ Divide the main items into the number of key people you have and delegate the tasks with a formal instruction that they sign.

☞ They can also delegate it down another level to the people who actually work with the items. For example, the forklift driver must do a daily inspection on the hydraulic hoses, chains and much more before he uses the forklift.

Below is a sample of a company manufacturing roof trusses. You will see how the management delegated the safety down to the workers.

Assigned Occupation, Health and Safety duties (Courtesy of Rooftek, Strand South Africa)

Management		Factory staff			
Oversee:		**Duties:**		**Duties:**	
Kalahari	Plant Maintenance	**Samual**	Safety measures on web cutter	**Pieter**	Inspection of fire fighting equipment
	Lifting Equipment		Maintenance of web cutter		Forklifts operating
	Noise and light		Protective equipment		Stacking of timber
	Fire precautions		Housekeeping		Housekeeping
	Electrical certificate of compliance		Report incidents		
	Subcontractors indemnity				
	Training and records				
Henk	Safety on Machines	**Llewellyn**	Safety measures on cross cut saws	**At**	Maintenance and safety measures of hoist and crane
	First aid		Maintenance on cross cut saws		
	Protective equipment		Protective equipment		Safety of delivery staff
	Incident register		Forklift operating and stacking of timber		Protective equipment
	Admin of legal requirements		Housekeeping		Housekeeping
			Report incidents		Report incidents
Eben	Oversee duties of factory staff	**Willie**	Safety measures on roller press		
	Hoisting equipment certificates		Maintenance of roller press		
	Operator certificates		Protective equipment		
	Stacking of timber approvals		Forklift operator + stacking of timber		
	Safety of high risk machines		Housekeeping		
	Safety of portable electric equipment		Report incidents		
	Housekeeping\				
	Accident investigation			This is just a portion of the OHS task list	

Checks to make sure you have the benefit of this chapter:

	Yes	No
I will walk around daily and point out dirt and untidy items to my staff:	☐	☐
I will demand tidiness from my staff all the time:	☐	☐
I will have safety talks regularly, with or without a formal safety program:	☐	☐
I will allow no jokes or horseplay and discipline harshly to stop it:	☐	☐
I will do all I can to ensure a safe workplace for myself and my staff:	☐	☐

11

Managing finances

There are several resources in a company and we have dealt with them earlier in the 6M's theory. These were Money, Management, Methods, Machines, Manpower and Materials. You have to understand each one of them. This chapter will help you deal with the responsibilities concerning money and finances.

Everything you do costs money. Workers get salaries, raw materials have to be paid for, machines needs electricity or fuel to run and attracts a cost per running hour because of maintenance and other costs. The management of the company where you work must be in control of all the costs. To be in control there are a few things they do:

- They draw up a sales plan.
- The calculate how much raw materials, salaries, electricity, maintenance, marketing expenses, all kinds of services and whatever else they need will cost in order to sell the sales plan.
- They draw up a budget using the above calculations.
- They rely on the managers to do all the right activities so that the budget is executed as closely as possible.

What is a budget?
A budget is a financial plan and it must include all the money you need to make the products or services you sell as well as the money that is expected from the sales of the products or services. The budget

estimates how great the profit or loss for your company will be for a specific period (normally 12 months)

> Note about spending:
>
> The budget is not the target amount to spend.

Where do you fit into the new budget?

The CEO (Chief Executive Officer) of your company cannot know all the detail of every department and cannot draw up a budget on your behalf. In very small companies and private businesses, this may be possible. The senior management needs your inputs in order to draw up the company budget. Your inputs must be as accurate as possible. I know you cannot predict the future, but you can take the past into consideration and estimate the future based on the production plan or budget. We will discuss how to do it in this chapter.

Last, but not least, you must execute the present budget with responsibility and deal with deviations.

Making a budget:

Gathering information:

Each company has a different financial budget start and finish date. For example, some start in January and finish in December, and others could start in July and finish in June the next year.

Do not wait for the end of the year to gather the information that you need for the budget of the next year. As a manager or supervisor you must do monthly reports. Make sure these reports cover the 6M's (Money, Management, Methods, Machines, Manpower and Materials) as well as the production figures. Some of those have costs assigned to them that you can use in development of the new budget.

<u>Different Budget elements:</u>
We distinguish against an operating budget and capital budget.

☞ Operating budget defines the daily operating costs we will incur in our departments to produce the items required to be sold.

☞ Capital budgets will define capital items required such as plant and machinery, land and buildings and vehicles to be used in the business over an extended period

<u>Budget assumptions:</u>
It's important to understand what assumptions have been made by the management and Finance department in developing the budget. Sales volumes, price increases, salary and wage increases, depreciation rates, production volumes etcetera will normally be defined upfront and, if they haven't been, it's important that you list the assumptions you have used in your calculations. For example: machines required will require capital expenditure.

Once the basic assumptions, such as number of units, selling price and inflation, as well as capacity/output of machinery, have been defined you will be required to budget your department costs. Where your area of management is will dictate how much of the budget you will have to do.

<u>Note:</u>
We will focus the Operating budget and review the different cost elements below.

<u>Calculate the "Direct cost per item":</u>
I use cost per item in the budget example because we assume the company you work for sells something or "items". The "items" can be cars, pipes, parts, a liquid measured by volume or by weight, hours (consultants and lawyers for example) and much more.

Your department will be responsible for managing certain costs and the information you gather every month can be used to make and report against the budget. The best way to explain it is by reviewing a specific example below for an actual month, where "cost" represents your currency, for example Dollar, Euro, South African Rand or anything else:

Month:	April 2011	Cost	% of total cost
Management (Cost)	Your salary as well as the salaries of people in your department not directly responsible for the product, for example Quality Control, Maintenance etc	22345	2.2%
Manpower (Cost)	The total paid to the workers, including overtime.	44500	4.4%
Machines (Cost)	Maintenance cost and spare parts for machines, vehicles, cranes and equipment you use for producing the product.	5400	0.5%
Materials (Cost)	All raw materials as well as indirect materials like safety clothes, consumables, etc.	941450	92.9%
	Total cost:	1013695	100%
Products (Number of Items)		8675 Items	
	Cost per item:	116.85	

Notes:

1. The cost is based on the volumes produced and based on direct costs only.

2. If half the number of products is made next year the cost per item will be very different because the management, manpower and machine cost may be the same, not half. Recalculate the cost per item if this is the case.

3. Calculate the percentage of every budget item related to the total (100%). You will use this to calculate the relative budgets from the sales budgets your management will provide you.

<u>Calculate the "Indirect cost per item"</u>
Indirect costs can be the following:

building rent, phones, electricity, marketing, stationary, senior management, royalties and much more. For the purpose of the explanation I have not made a budget for these items because it will just be duplication. If there are indirect items under your management you will have to budget for them.

<u>Make a first estimate of the budget per month for next year based on April.</u>
Management has bought another production machine and will start producing 2725 more items per month from next year. This will mean you need more people and several other things. The first thing you have to do is to use the above cost per item to get a rough estimate of the input costs. You calculate this as per the sample below:

Monthly budget for next year. The first estimate.			1st estimate Budget
a.)	Cost per item this year	116.85	
b.)	Cost per item with inflation of 3.5% (116.85 x (1 + 3.5/100))	120.94	
c.)	Items to make next year - Sales budget from Management (8675 last year +2725 more for next year)	11400	
Next year's total budget (c x b)		100%	1378742
Management (1378742 x 2.2 / 100)		2.2%	30332
Manpower (1378742 x 4.4 / 100)		4.4%	60665
Machines (1378742 x 0.5 / 100)		0.5%	6894
Materials (1378742 x 92.9 / 100)		92.9%	1280851

<u>Make a second estimate of the budget per month for next year based on April.</u>

The cost per unit will be relatively the same, apart from inflation, if the production is approximately the same. If the sales are much less and the number of people and machines stay the same your calculations will be very wrong.

In our case there will be another machine and a lot more items per month. The fact that you used the extra production to estimate the new budget will automatically increase all the inputs, but it may not be so simple because the inputs may not scale up in the same way.

You must now look carefully at the following budgets:

1. Management: Can the same QC staff and you manage an extra machine? Will you need more maintenance workers? If so, the cost of management will just be adjusted with the new salaries next year, not scaled up by the extra production.

2. Manpower: Do you need more people for the extra machine? Will you spend more on training because you have new workers?

3. Machines: Will you spend more on maintenance?

4. Materials: We used the estimated inflation, which is the consumer price index issued by the government based on household items. Raw materials may be subject to shortages, sanctions, political problems, over supply or something that will change the price. Make sure you have a good estimate of the price and adjust the budget accordingly.

5. Cost per item: Before you start calculating in a loop, start with the price increase for next year. The sales department will provide it. In our example this is 3.5%, the consumer price index, because the items you make are sold to the public and it fits in with food and other items. Use this inflated value for the

new per unit input cost and then adjust the input as per specific costs like one of the raw materials. Specific items might have exceeded the normal inflation values and they will need special adjustment.

6. To work out the new raw material budget you must calculate the raw material quantity per item. Your present actual costs will help you do it. Then apply the new estimated cost to the item and get the new price of the raw materials.

7. The new budget for our example is listed below. You will make more items with just two extra workers. The input cost is less because one of the main raw materials has an oversupply. Your management took advantage of this and bought another machine to produce more items. You will see that the new item cost is only 96.85 (1104035 / 1140 = 96.85). The company will have a better profit margin and will make some extra money next year.

8. What is also interesting to note is that the building and other overhead costs do not increase if you make more products. In our example the same building, the same management, using the same offices, will be there if you make more products or not. The fact that indirect costs do not increase will bring down the item cost as well. Remember this is an example to help you think through the aspects that make a budget; it is not necessarily a good example.

2nd monthly estimate for budget for next year	Budget
Quantity of items to make per month next year - Sales budget from Management	11400
Next year's budget per month	1104035
Management (the same people adjusted for inflation)	23127
Manpower (2 more workers and adjusted for inflation)	49162.5
Machines (increase by extra item cost)	6894
Materials (Main raw material is cheaper next year because of over supply)	1024851

<u>Case study: Budget:</u>

I worked for a semi-government organisation in 1991. In the last quarter of the financial year our Department Manager called a meeting and addressed all the staff. In *this* meeting he told us that we still had ZAR25 million to spend before the financial year ended and that we must pull out all the stops. It sounded wrong at the time and it sounds ridiculous now.

What do we learn from this story?:

- The budget is not the amount of money to spend.

- There is work to be done for which there is budgeted money to pay for raw materials, manpower, overheads, development, research and so on.

- If you did all the work and there is still some money in the budget, report it as such. You may even get a tap on the shoulder for management of the budget.

Managing the budget:

The budget is a plan, like any other and like the plan you have for production, training and so on. In this case the plan addresses financial issues. You must stick to the plan as far as possible with the following in mind:

The plan was estimated by yourself and others who guessed the future and therefore it must be re-evaluated all the time as you see the "future" unfolding.

General finance management:

The budget is a management tool, it is a plan. While executing this plan you'll deal with other finance issues.

<u>Cash flow:</u>

Cash is king!! Without cash, no business can survive. The company will most likely not have a lot of cash in the bank. There are invoices that customers will pay that will bring in cash and there will be raw materials, salaries and many other things that must be paid and that will spend the cash coming in. Sometimes the incoming cash is slower than the cash going out because you make the product before you sell it. The financial manager, or somebody else, will manage this cash flow. Your job is to make sure they know how much you will spend and when you need the goods or service. In some cases the company will borrow the cash from the bank and pay interest while they wait for the invoices to be paid. Unnecessary spending in this case is very costly. The budget is one of the tools to manage the cash.

> Remember the budget is not a target.
>
> You don't have to spend all the money or incur all the costs you have forecasted. The budget is rather a monitoring tool to measure your actual cost against estimated cost and a mechanism to determine if you are going to make the projected profit. **This will be an indicator for the management to help you** if you are not making it.

Execute the budget:

Take a look at the plan in the beginning of every month and make sure it is relevant. Sometimes expansions are in the budget, but the sales did not realise and the management does not want to expand any more. They may not tell you; you have to ask.

☞ If you need to do things to get the work done that is on the budget you need to plan the work, get spending approvals and so on in due time. Plan ahead.

☞ If you need to appoint people as part of the budget plan, make sure you start well in advance because if the salary of the new worker appears on the budget in April, you will have to start the recruitment process in February or earlier.

☞ Upgrades and major overhauls of machines and processes may be on the budget for a particular month, but you need to start the activity in the months before.

Purchase requisitions:

Make sure everything you buy is formally requested and signed off by the right authority. In modern systems this is all done by a computer system that will check if the item you buy is budgeted or not. This will determine the level of approval. A purchase request will be handled by the buyer and the delivery as well as payment options will be negotiated so there are no cash flow surprises.

Scrap:
Scrap is waste and a loss, but the raw materials that made the scrap must be replaced. Make sure you record all scrap and order the replacement materials and adjust your budget accordingly. This must include the approval of your senior management.

Control spending:
In an earlier chapter I told the story of a manager who insisted that he sign all the cheques and money transfers, all payments in other words. He actually thought he controlled the spending. He was wrong, because others controlled the use of spare parts and raw materials and he could only stop unnecessary spending of non-production items that must be paid for before delivery.

To control the spending you must control the people and machines that apply the materials and make sure they ask your approval BEFORE they apply the spares or materials. This kind of approval can only be managed if a system with various approval and/or authority levels is introduced in all departments.

Continued improvement:
Profit = Income – spending. Your company owes its existence to the fact that it wants to make a profit for its owners. Non-profit organisations have other objectives as well, like job creation, service to mankind, uplifting the community, service to the community or members and much more. Whatever the reason, they want more for a lower cost. Your job is to find ways to improve the production of the items (goods or services or whatever) as well as reduce the input costs. Study every process and method and read on the subject. Every small step in the right direction has an impact on the whole.

Financial pitfalls:

Saving money:

You will be expected to save money and make sure your workers save money as well. "Saving money" is a loose term that actually means you must not waste any money. I have never seen anybody in my life in any company I worked for that passed money to the company savings account. It simply means: "Waste nothing".

Normally, people will not waste money on purpose, but people may neglect to make special efforts not to waste anything that costs money if they realise this effort is not appreciated or if they see the management wasting the money they "save".

Policy:

Whenever there is a shortage of cash there will be policies to regulate spending. These can be:

- ☞ Everybody flies in economy class,
- ☞ The CEO must sign all expenditure approvals,
- ☞ Nobody gets a computer upgrade,
- ☞ It is not allowed to buy new tools,
- ☞ and many more...

There is nothing wrong with these policies, but individual cases may require that the policy be ignored and common sense be applied because following the policy will actually cost more. I will quote one example that I was involved in as a young engineer: A drilling machine broke. It had to be replaced, but we were not allowed to buy new tools. We had it repaired at nearly double the cost of a new one. Yes, you are right, it is ridiculous, but it happened and the "money saving" policy did not save anything. No matter what we did, the management stuck to the policy.

> It's your role to highlight specific examples to management if you believe the policy needs to be adjusted, even for a single case. DO NOT simply violate company policy.

Re-using scrap:

Scrap is not a free material. If you recover raw material from scrap, this raw material is actually more expensive than it was when it was new because it was processed by machines and people who were paid. It is better to re-use the material than to throw it away and in that sense it is a "free" material. Your job is to minimise scrap to as near to zero as possible. Remember that prevention is always better that cure.

> Only a fool will say: "Don't worry, we can re-use the scrap".

Measure:

Budgets are not controlled unless actual cost is measured against the original budget. Report any overspend and or savings as this will allow for better forecasts going forward.

Never too small:

Never underestimate the value of a small cost saving. If the small savings are overlooked the total impact could be lost. If you can save a number of small savings it will result in a big saving when combined. Encourage all your employees to make suggestions and contribute with ideas to save money. Keep a record of the savings you made as it will benefit your department if you can prove you have managed your department's finances well.

Cheaper is not always better:

Be careful not to always go for the cheapest product as the quality might be below standard and might impact your production throughput and or the quality of your final product.

> The bitterness of poor quality lingers on long after the sweetness of cheap prices is forgotten.
>
> The author of this quote is unknown

Do not buy from only one supplier:

Companies often encounter problems if they only procure from one supplier. If you don't check prices regularly with other suppliers you might find that your supplier prices are no longer competitive. It is a good practice to get quotations from more than one supplier. This function might fall under your procurement department but if you know of a better supplier it is important that you disclose this information.

Home finances:

Learn to manage your finances at home. Live within your means. Draft a plan (in our case we call this a budget). Stick to the plan, even if your friend sells his car for half what it is worth and you miss the bargain of a lifetime. If your home finances are a mess, you may struggle to manage the finances at work. Fix it as soon as possible.

> A bargain is not a bargain unless you planned to buy it before you knew about it and only if you really need it.

<u>**Case Study: My sons and their budgets**</u>

To teach my children about how to manage money I waited for each of them to finish school. After school they were grown-ups in our eyes. From this *time* onwards, we expected them to be responsible with money and many other things.

Now, at the time of writing this book, we have three children at university. We decided to let them manage their own finances. It started with the oldest son and it worked well. Then we implemented it for each child as they started their studies.

This is what we did:

We asked them to prepare a budget and we helped them to list all the expenses they knew of. This included class fees, hostel fees, books, pocket money, travel costs, etc. They drew up a spreadsheet with columns Jan–Dec (we are in the Southern hemisphere where the school year runs Jan-Dec). In the spreadsheet, each month's column had "budget" and "actual". I paid the money into their accounts for the next months according to the budget they produced. It worked well. They paid the university, the hostel, bought books, took pocket money and so on as per the financial plan.

Sometimes the plan was wrong and the expenses were more or less. In this case, they had a budget revision meeting with us and we approved the new budget.

In order for them to receive the money for the next period, they have to give me the balanced spreadsheet of the past period. I need proof of payment for every expenditure, except their pocket money. I do not care what they do with their pocket money, unless I think they are wasting it, then I will ask.

This works very well. They have proved to their parents that they can manage the money in their care. We hope that they will manage their home finances as well as work finances in the same responsible way.

Checks to make sure you have the benefit of this chapter:

Yes No

I will find the existing budget and study it: ☐ ☐

I will use the monthly report system to see if the budget is followed: ☐ ☐

If the budget is not followed, I will meet with the relevant managers and re-plan the budget under my management: ☐ ☐

I will do my best to help with the new budget and keep notes on expenditures to be able to make a fair forecast of what we will spend next year: ☐ ☐

I will do everything in my power not to waste any resources (money): ☐ ☐

I will manage the workers not to waste any resources: ☐ ☐

I will not ask of my workers what I do not do myself: ☐ ☐

12

Problem solving

It is amazing how little formal training is allocated to this subject, yet most managers spend the better portion of the day solving all kinds of problems.

As an engineer I have to solve problems all the time, mostly technical or production related. I was not very good at it and made some effort to study the subject. I was excited about how much more efficient I got at identifying the causes of problems. I told my wife about it. As I explained the method of effective problem solving to her, she told me that she had learned this as a physiotherapy student. I was impressed. The medical profession uses these techniques simply because they are solving problems all the time. As a physiotherapist my wife must find out why a patient has a problem in just a few minutes. Why is it then that engineers do not study it as a subject, together with mathematics, strength of materials and so forth? I do not know. It could be possible that the technical institutions of learning do not want to realise that most of their students will end up in management and other positions where they will solve problems almost all the time.

People have been solving problems since their childhood. Not everybody does it with the same efficiency. There is a method you can use. This method will not be anything new to you, just rearrange the order in which you solved problems anyway.

How is problem solving most likely done now?:

Firstly, something goes wrong, gets out of place, works differently, breaks, gets lost, and so on, either by itself, by some outside or inside influence, or by a person.

Secondly, we usually see the problem created by the above and jump to some conclusion that seems obvious.

Thirdly, in many cases the person with most influence has the best solution because he has the biggest platform from which to announce the solution. The problem is most likely not solved in the first round and only then do we start gathering facts, start analysing, look at trends, involving other people and so forth, until we stumble onto the solution. It is better to have a method.

Describe the problem:

Write down what the problem is or what equipment has a problem. Write down what is wrong with it, or what it stopped doing or what it is doing differently. Once you've done that, analyse what you wrote and test it to see if it is clear. Add detail of what it was before, when the problem occurred, what the symptoms are, what else is affected and whatever you find. Once you are done you have a PROBLEM STATEMENT.

The basic method of listing possible causes:

1. Describe the problem.

2. Do not jump to immediate conclusions and quick fixes. If time allows it, take note of the situation and gather some facts, not opinions.

3. Ask the question: "What was the condition or situation before the problem started?"

4. Ask this until you have all the answers.

5. Ask the question: "What changed" from the time all was OK until the time there was a problem.

6. Keep asking "what changed" until you have the smallest item that has changed from the time there was no problem to the time when the problem started.

7. Write next to each possible cause how it could have caused the problem.

8. Ask what would be likely if there were more of these changes or less of these changes and note your answers.

9. Look at the causes and, for each one, ask "if this was the cause, would other things also have gone wrong?"

10. Use a person as an advisor on the problem solving team who is not deeply involved in the problem so that you will get an objective approach.

11. Keep on repeating this loop until you find the problem.

> Keep asking: WHAT CHANGED?

Apply maintenance principles to the problem:
If one part in a system breaks down or something was responsible for a problem, it is possible that the same cause can be present in other similar parts. Look at the following examples to get this point more clearly:

☞ If a hydraulic hose leaks, it is possible that there are more hoses that are as old, or undergo the same amount of bending or rub against the same structure. Investigate and replace all of them as a preventative measure.

☞ If an electrical part fails, look for other parts connected to the same source and apply the same protection.

☞ If a raw material caused the problem, find all places where this material and other material from the same supplier are used and make sure there are no deviations in the quality. Suppliers of raw materials often change the make-up of their products as they hunt for cheaper and alternative materials. They claim the products are the same, but the new material, combined with other materials in your process can cause a problem. This is especially relevant in products like chemicals, paints, resins and so forth.

☞ Mechanical items like chains, drives, gearboxes, bearings all have a life span between services and if neglected will fail. If one fails the others may follow soon.

<u>Case Study: My Nissan Patrol:</u>

In 1998, while living in Botswana, I bought a second hand Nissan Patrol 4.2 litre Diesel station wagon. It is a fantastic 4x4 and we drove all over *the* game reserves with it. Much later, when it had about 180 000 km on the clock, I heard a noise and found that the water pump had failed. I replaced it. 15000 km later I was driving on the highway between Johannesburg and Pretoria when the car just slowed down to a stop. The red light told me the car had just overheated. The engine had in fact ceased. I had to overhaul it. In the process of overhauling it, the mechanic showed me the part that held the thermostat. A hole was corroded in the aluminium and had caused the water to short circuit back to the engine instead of being pumped through the radiator to cool it down. A second problem was that the radiator, a horizontal type, was blocked from two-thirds down. I replaced the aluminium and had the radiator serviced and cleaned.

Could this have been prevented? YES. How?

• Firstly, the agents who serviced the car should have drained and replaced the cooling water every ten or twenty thousand kilometres because it becomes an acid over time that eats the aluminium, but this is not the real prevention.

- When the water pump broke down, I should have looked beyond the fix and asked what other parts in the same system could be as aged, or have experienced the same abuse, or used the same system as the water pump. These are the thermostat, the radiator and the hoses.

- If I had had those checked by a workshop specializing in cooling systems when the water pump failed, I could have saved myself a lot of money.

- IMPORTANT: You may think less of me for driving an old car and that I should expect it to break down, BUT in your place of work, the machines, buildings, people and many other things you manage will not be replaced with new ones every three years. Therefore this story has a huge significance to you as a manager.

Examples of items that can cause big problems:

☞ Suppliers of raw materials can change one of the ingredients or properties of a material.

☞ An operator can change a setting on the machine.

☞ A new rule could have been implemented or followed.

☞ A new or different procedure could have been implemented or followed.

☞ A new staff member on the job.

☞ A new manager in charge.

☞ A new machine doing some of the work.

☞ A worn part.

☞ Neglected maintenance: a part that should have been changed but was not.

From the chapter on Management TOOLS:

The following tools are part of this chapter. You must study them in order to improve or solve your problems related to production, efficiency and other non-tangible long-term problems.

1.	TOP 5

2.	Cause-Remedy book or databases

Checks to see if you have the benefit this chapter:

Yes   No

I will not jump to the first obvious conclusion: ☐ ☐

I will make a list of questions to ask whenever I must solve a problem. This list will help me not to jump to conclusions: ☐ ☐

I will test every possible solution by asking "if more of.." or "if less of ...": ☐ ☐

After a problem is solved I will give feedback to others who may have similar problems because they use similar machines or work in similar conditions. I will do all I can to prevent a similar problem in the future: ☐ ☐

I will train people to cope with the problem or similar problems in future: ☐ ☐

13

Discipline and legal procedures

Lets start with a definition of discipline:

http://en.wikipedia.org/wiki/Discipline states: "In its original sense, 'discipline' is the systematic instruction given to 'disciples' to train them as students in a craft or trade, or to follow a particular code of conduct or 'order'. Often, the phrase 'to discipline' carries a negative connotation. This is because enforcement of order – that is, ensuring instructions are carried out – is often regulated through punishment".

It simply means that you know how to do your job and how to behave. This includes submitting to a set of rules and other guidelines set by your company, your country, your parents, your family or yourself.

The first rule you must follow is that you must give your company what they pay for, normally 'work'.

Some rules are laws and therefore cannot be disregarded, negotiated or ignored.

If you respect the rules and laws applicable to your work and do your work well and correctly there should be no problems. You must also behave in the correct manner and respect others.

If a person fails to do his work as was agreed or he misbehaves, or breaks the rules or laws, he will be in trouble. Your staff must know and obey the rules just like any other person. You need to make sure they know the rules and obey them because you will have to discipline them if they overstep the mark. It is needless to say that you must set an example and therefore you must know and obey the rules better than everybody else.

Common discipline problems:
- Late coming
- Not performing assigned duties, but doing other work
- Under the influence of alcohol. This includes arriving intoxicated from the previous night's drinking or drinking during business hours, for example during lunch.
- Doing private work
- Unauthorised union activities (meetings, go-slow, strike etc.)
- Taking and/or giving bribes
- Stealing
- Sexual harassment
- Sabotage
- Practical jokes
- Absence without leave
- Corruption
- Insubordination
- Assaulting another worker
- Disregard for company code of conduct
- Dishonesty

Know the rules:

Get a copy of the company rules and study them carefully. You must have an intimate knowledge of the rules. Make sure your staff knows the rules. Do not let people overstep or disregard unimportant rules. This will be like cooking the proverbial frog alive. In the frog's case the water temperature is raised slowly so that the frog gets used to the higher temperature. Then the temperature is put higher and higher until it is happy to be cooked. If your staff gets away with breaking unimportant rules, they will start breaking more rules and more serious rules. You will not know when to start disciplining them until it is too late. You need to have a ZERO tolerance approach. It is a well-known fact that if you are strict on petty things the big issues look after themselves.

Apply the rules in the same way to all the staff. This includes any family who may work for you. Just be strict and firm and it will pay off in the long run.

Correcting behaviour:

If a worker does something wrong you must make sure he knows the correct behaviour and try your best to get the person to change. In some cases there are no-tolerance rules and you have to dismiss the worker. Your company will, or should, have a list of these behaviours.

A guideline to follow is that of a father who disciplines his children. He cannot fire or dismiss his children and must therefore handle misbehaviour in a way that will help his child to correct that particular behaviour. He does not want to lose or distance the child from himself in the process. In the same way, you must discipline workers with the intent to correct their behaviour. Do not keep firing everybody because you will soon find yourself amongst fresh workers who don't have the experience to perform to a high standard.

Apply the following rules when you discipline workers:
1. Tell a worker if he does something wrong. Explain the correct way to do it. Make a note and let him sign it.

2. If it is a serious mistake, you must follow disciplinary procedures and have a formal hearing, with an outcome that can be the issuing of a verbal warning, written warning or whatever the chairman of the meeting decides. Keep this record on the worker's file.

3. Always keep in mind that your first and most important duty is to correct the wrong behaviour.

4. If the same worker keeps on breaking rules or does not do his job right and does not respond to your correction or your help, he will get himself into a position where he dismisses himself. This way you will not fire him, he will fire himself.

5. Make sure you have a very good record of everything because the person may take you to the labour court in which case you will have to prove that it was a fair dismissal.

6. Do not use the disciplinary system to get rid of people.

> In a disciplinary action, you must deal with the CONDUCT of the worker, not his performance.

Case study: Senior management staff can also make mistakes, but..

In a company where I worked, one of the side loader drivers overturned the vehicle while reversing and turning too fast at the same time. A side loader *is* a purpose-built fork truck that handles longitudinal loads on its side. It is an awkward upright vehicle and should be driven with care. The vehicle was empty. In the disciplinary enquiry the driver almost lost his job with a final written warning against his name. The value of the damage was 20000 Botswana Pula.(about US$3000) The insurance covered the damage.

Not long after this accident, a senior manager had to fly to Johannesburg. When he got out of his car at the airport he removed his briefcase from the back seat of his car on the driver side and put it in the street behind him while getting his overnight bag. A passing car ran over the briefcase, which had a 25000 Botswana Pula Notebook computer inside it, a lot of money in 2001. He realized that he had backups and dumped the damaged Notebook PC, bag and all, in the nearest rubbish bin. There was no inquiry, no discipline hearing no problem. The insurance covered the damage.

What do we learn from this story?

- Rules apply to everybody and the extent of negligence cannot be established by the guilty party.

- Never do your own investigations. The workforce will hear of these things and can be de-motivated, discouraged and angry if there are two sets of rules, one for them and one for senior management.

Troublemakers:

There may be troublemakers on your staff. I suggest you think of them as runaway bull dozers. You cannot stop a runaway bull dozer by standing firm in its path. You have to jump up and grab the controls, to first of all guide it where you want it to go and do some ground levelling and then park it in a safe place with blocks behind the wheels or tracks.

I have been accused of being a troublemaker many times. Some times it was actually true. Maybe it is because I simply cannot go with the mainstream and definitely because I have been very frustrated in some of my jobs.

I have found that troublemakers have the following in common:

☞ They are usually intelligent,

☞ They are almost never employed to their full potential,

☞ They always start well and only become troublemakers later on,

☞ They are most likely frustrated.

☞ They are most likely involved in voluntary organisations where they may have high positions, for example the unions.

Dealing with troublemakers:

☞ Get some background to determine his motivation.

☞ Try to establish his intelligence and abilities, for example his qualifications, how fast he understands new things, etc.

☞ Determine if he is frustrated or angry.

☞ Deal with the problem by letting him make suggestions.

☞ In most cases you will find that the person is generally good, but under utilised. Give him more responsibility and monitor the situation carefully. Then give more if he takes to it. If you cannot change the person and nothing else works, you will have to get rid of him or her if the person does not leave on his own. That person can have a negative effect on your other staff and the performance of your output.

☞ Remember what was said in the first chapter about "People leave people, not companies". Have a hard look at yourself. Maybe you must change if more and more people on your team seem to be "troublemakers".

Checks to see if I have the benefit of this chapter:

	Yes	No
I will create an environment where people will follow the rules because it is the right thing to do:	☐	☐
I will be an example of how to conduct oneself and how to obey the rules and regulations of the company:	☐	☐
I will not use the legal system to get rid of people I do not like, but will rather try to adapt things so that the person can fit in:	☐	☐
I will make a record of all discussions and disciplinary procedures with my staff and file it in their personnel files:	☐	☐
I will apply all rules in the same way to all people:	☐	☐
I will make a study of every troublemaker and see if there is something that I can do to lessen the reason for frustration, under-utilisation or whatever it is that aggravated the person:	☐	☐

14

Acknowledgements and appreciation

Writing this book was no easy task. It reflects knowledge and experience. Needless to say I have studied and applied what I saw in nature as well as what I've read in books, learned in seminars, from colleagues, from my family, from other managers, from leaders and what I experienced over many years. I have learned a lot from those who have managed me well, noting their methods so that I could copy them. I have also learned a lot from those who mismanaged, abused and frustrated me by observing them and noting the effect it had. I always searched for better ways to manage people and processes.

I did not copy any book, nor did I steal any concepts or ideas that are original or copyrighted to any other author or person. Where I did copy something, I gave credit for it.

I fully appreciate the work and inputs from all those who have shaped my experience and knowledge. I have listed some of them below.

The seminars, workshops, study material and activities that influenced my knowledge of management are:

- ✔ The knowledge I have on the subject of social behaviour comes from seminars I attended on leadership and people skills. The chapters dealing with this subject are from my memory, interpretation and experience of what I was taught. I did not quote directly from the material I was given. I did not try to duplicate the courses and recommend that you attend seminars on the subject to improve your knowledge and application beyond what this book can provide. I give specific credit to the courses I attended and the material covered namely:

    - S Burger: I attended his seminar in 1986

    - Sanlam in-house training for sales people, who's naming of the styles I adapted and used after translating them into English. I attended this seminar in 1987.

    - Sharpening your people skills from WTB Inc (1989): I attended this seminar in 1995 as a self-funded leadership training in a volunteer organisation where I served.

- ✔ I attended a seminar on Problem Solving and Decision Making from Kepner & Tregoe in around 1995. This is where I was schooled in problem solving.

- ✔ I searched the internet on the subject of management and anything else when I had to find answers on specific topics. None of these are quoted directly here.

- ✔ Dr. John C Maxwell, whose seminar on leadership I attended in Hatfield, Pretoria. I read two of his books on leadership and teamwork, but did not quote directly from them. I inserted a blog post that references his book: Leadership Gold.

- ✔ Business Re-engineering: I was a member of the order fulfilment team of the re-engineering of Denel Somchem under the sponsorship of Coopers & Lybrand. This is where I learned about business mapping and many other valuable things like managing the A, B and C activities.

You may note that I do not have a long list of books I have read or referenced on the subject of management. So where does my knowledge come from, apart from the above list? Life is a school. Some call it the University of Hard Knocks. I am honoured to name a few of the people that shaped the experience and knowledge that I have today. I cannot mention every person and apologise if I missed somebody who feels they should have been mentioned. Mentioning a person's name does not mean he approves of anything I've written in this book.

The people that helped to shape my experience and knowledge of management are:

Note: The companies that I name next to the people are the companies these people worked for when I learned from them. Some of them have moved on since then.

<u>Juan Enrique Henning, my father</u> always said: "I will never sell my name for all the money in the world" and he never did. He was a man of integrity, a true teacher, using every opportunity to teach me something, from cooking to fixing a car, the finances of his business and just about everything he did. He was born of South African parents in Argentina. He spoke many Latin languages. At age nine he was the person to fix windmills in the Chubut area where they lived. At age eleven, in 1928, he figured out how the charger in their Ford model T worked and hooked up the generator to the windmill to make electric light in the kitchen for his mother. I can name many more stories of his technical genius, but that is for another forum.

<u>Elmar Henning, my mother</u> taught me not to accept the status quo or anything that is not what I wanted. From there comes my constant modifying of the things I buy. She also taught me to finish what I start. She is from a long line of innovators and grew up in a very different environment than I did here in South Africa. She was born in Indonesia of Dutch parents. Her father, Frans Tullingh, was a successful Dutch artist. He mother, Gesina Ozinga, studied arts and then accountancy

in France. She was probably one of the first female accountants in Holland in the early 1930s. My mother's grandfather, Klaas Ozinga, was an engineer on the first railway in the Transvaal, South Africa, the Ambassador for Holland and CEO for Shell in Romania in the late 1800s and early 1900s. Her aunt was one of the first female doctors in Holland. My mother has been, and still is, a great influence in my life.

<u>Deidré Henning, my wife:</u> She supports me and believes in what I do. My career has presented many challenges to her and our children. She and our children deserves medals. She challenges my theories to the point where they become part of my life or I discard them. She is great! We are a team.

<u>Hendrik, Bryan and Pieter Henning, our sons:</u> Each one of them communicates in a different style (see the chapters on team building for more information on this topic). It is in our family that I gained the most experience on the subject of communication. I wrote about them in some of the case studies. We are very proud of them.

<u>Maarten Henning:</u> Dairy Bell. He was my late uncle who shared his "management by walking around" experience with my father and me when we visited him at his factory where he took us on a tour. I saw firsthand what he meant.

<u>Custav Kotze:</u> Rupert International Technical Centre. He told me not to take over the responsibility from my manager if he did not do his job.

<u>Paul Cogan:</u> Rembrandt Tobacco Company. He modelled respect for fresh ideas and taught me that if you do a fantastic job, but do not wrap it well, or do not finish it off properly, your work cannot be appreciated.

<u>Mike Smyth:</u> Dairy Belle. He allowed me to find my own solutions and valued the results, giving me a lot of confidence as a young engineer.

Hennie Vorster: Sanlam. He was a colleague when I sold life insurance. He saw that I struggled with sales and took me to his office, gave me some money and a strategy to find and contact prospects that got me out of the slump. He demonstrated care and leadership in a way I have rarely seen before or since.

André Roodt: Ebed. He was my leader in the volunteer organisation where I worked in my spare time. He taught me to duplicate myself in others and work myself out of a job. He said if a leader has measles, the followers cannot have chickenpox. I learned the F.A.S.T. principle from him.

Willie Meissner: Denel Somchem. He was my manager and had to put up with me, who was oblivious to the rules in a weapons manufacturing facility. He modelled great leadership attributes. For example: I had some ideas that he thought were great and he arranged for me to present them to the senior management. He had no interest in taking credit for my ideas. Trust me, this is rarely seen in the field of engineering. He is a motivator of note and is an example to me and others.

Michael Crocker: Denel Somchem. He was my colleague, later my manager. He modelled respect for others and integrity. He uplifted and taught the staff all the time. He respected the lowest rank as he respected the MD. He is an example on the subject of managing production, safety and housekeeping.

Nico Heyns (Gryskop Nico): Denel Somchem. He had a huge respect for me as a person and for my technical abilities in a place where it was not the norm. It took me a while to see he was for real. He was a true scientist, manager, role model and friend to many. He has passed away now, a loss to us all.

Dr. König: Plessey South Africa. He explained the importance of managing the "middle manager" because they spend the raw materials and therefore the money, as well as managing most of the company's biggest asset, its people. As the MD of a big company, most of his time and effort were spent on this group of managers. He also taught me the curved-ball theory.

<u>Thys Neethling:</u> University of Stellenbosch. He was one of the mentors I consulted when I did not know what to do with situations at work. Some of the advice he gave me has been passed onto others with great effect. He taught me to stand back and see the "wood for the trees" regarding my work situation.

<u>Bryan Lemar:</u> Owens Corning Pipe Botswana. He modelled integrity, honesty and respect for others and taught me a lot of people skills. He gave me freedom to do my work with a 100% confidence in me. I used this opportunity to grow and develop my management skills.

<u>Agnar Gilbu:</u> Flowtite. Being involved with senior people gave me insight into proven management methods. In this case good solid honesty, no tricks, no extreme theories, just hard work and clear goals.

<u>Doug Barker:</u> Owens Corning. He appointed me to solve the technical problems in a pipe factory in Botswana. As a senior executive of a USA top 500 company, he was not afraid to get involved in the lowest levels of our factory to assist the management, including me, to solve our problems. The "Top 5" tool comes from him. He used my office as a base when he visited and enjoyed telling me stories about his experiences from which I learned. Together we schemed and planned some of the solutions to the problems that faced our factory.

<u>Michael H Thaman:</u> Owens Corning: He taught me to use the implemented systems to the full potential, focus on the core activities, and always improve whatever I do - one sure step at a time. He looked for improvements on the factory floor, not in reports. He taught me not to let perfection stand in the way of something very good. This philosophy became a way of life for me and I applied this principle in my family and work ever since.

<u>Fernando Carreira:</u> Amitech South Africa. I was his manager for four years and learned a lot from him in the area of management simply because his feedback to me was always critical and uplifting, helping me to adjust and try new approaches.

Special thanks to the following people who verified and contested the content of this book to help me to make it something useful. Some of them actually applied and tested the concepts before commenting.

- ✔ Deidré Henning: physiotherapist, pre-school teacher, high school teacher, mother, wife and dear friend. She helped me to say things right and to say the right things.
- ✔ Waldi Lübbe: MBA graduate with a wide experience in management who made several edifying remarks.
- ✔ Gerjo Ben van der Merwe: Manager and partner of a manufacturing company. His feedback was very practical and had a big influence on the book in terms of the practical advice inside the chapters.
- ✔ Dirk Steinberg (CA)SA: Commercial Director, Genrec Engineering (Pty) Ltd, A Murray & Roberts Group Company. One of the first to comment in 2004, saying: "I already use some of the principles found in the book". Thank you also for your recent evaluation of the financial chapter.
- ✔ Dries and Andries Harmse: Owners of a manufacturing company.
- ✔ Bryan and Dirkie Muller for the first editing.
- ✔ Henk Lamprecht and the Rooftek team (Eben Groenewald and Kalahari) who used the book to "test" it.
- ✔ Stephan Pretoruis: Human Resources Consultant who gave me valuable comments.
- ✔ Iaan Jooste, JC Vorster, Mariana Lübbe, Dawie Harmse, André du Plessis and Giulio Santi who read and "tested" the book's concepts and theories.

✔ Several others, who advised, motivated and helped in some way or another to complete this book.

Finally, all glory to God.

<u>Special request to you, the reader:</u>

Please give me feedback after you have applied what you learned from this book. I'm not looking for praise; I'm looking for the following:

- ☐ Is everything well explained?
- ☐ I want to improve the knowledge base and share the experiences of others with more readers and students of the subject of management. Please give feedback and tell me your stories.
- ☐ I need to know if there are any topics you would like me to cover in the follow-up edition.
- ☐ I also want to have an active web site where you can get more information and where experiences of the readers can be shared.

15

Finally:

My son Bryan has sent me this story. It has particular interest to me because I am an Engineer who wrote on the subject of management. Enjoy it - THEN THINK!

A man in a hot air balloon realised he was lost. He reduced altitude and spotted a woman below. He descended a bit more and shouted, "Excuse me, can you help me? I promised a friend I would meet him an hour ago, but I don't know where I am."

The woman below replied, "You are in a hot air balloon hovering approximately thirty feet above the ground. You are between forty and forty-one degrees north latitude and between fifty-nine and sixty degrees west longitude."

"You must be an engineer," said the balloonist.

"I am," replied the woman, "How did you know?"

"Well," answered the balloonist, "everything you told me is technically correct, but I have no idea what to make of your information, and the fact is I am still lost. Frankly, you've not been much help so far."

The woman below responded, "You must be in management."

"I am," replied The balloonist, "but how did you know?"

"Well," said the woman, "you don't know where you are or where you are going. You have risen to where you are due to a large quantity of hot air. You made a promise, which you have no idea how to keep, and you expect people beneath you to solve your problems. The fact is you are in exactly the same position you were in before we met, but now, somehow, it's my fault."

Credits: The source is unknown. My appreciation to the author.